Real World
Colouring Book
For Advanced Users & Adults

50 Images

Created From Real Life Photos For You To Colour As You Please.

ISBN 978-0-359-97233-3

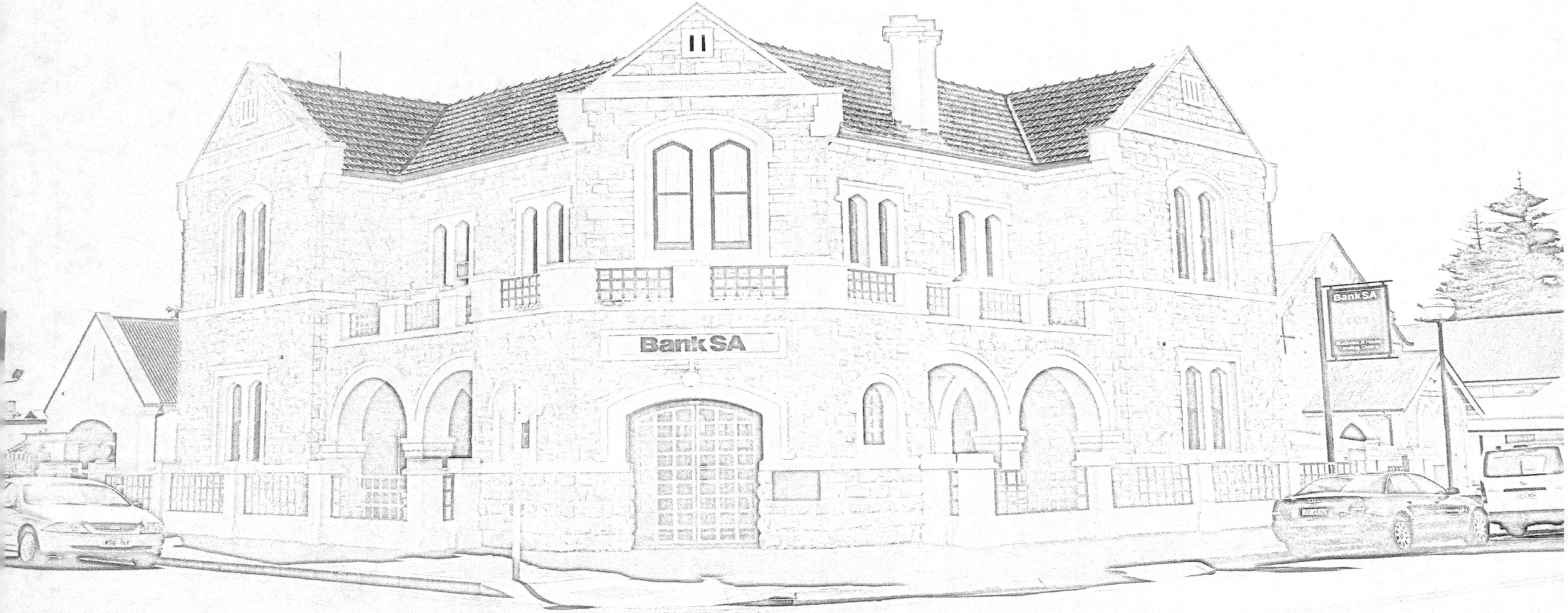
Bank SA
BankSA

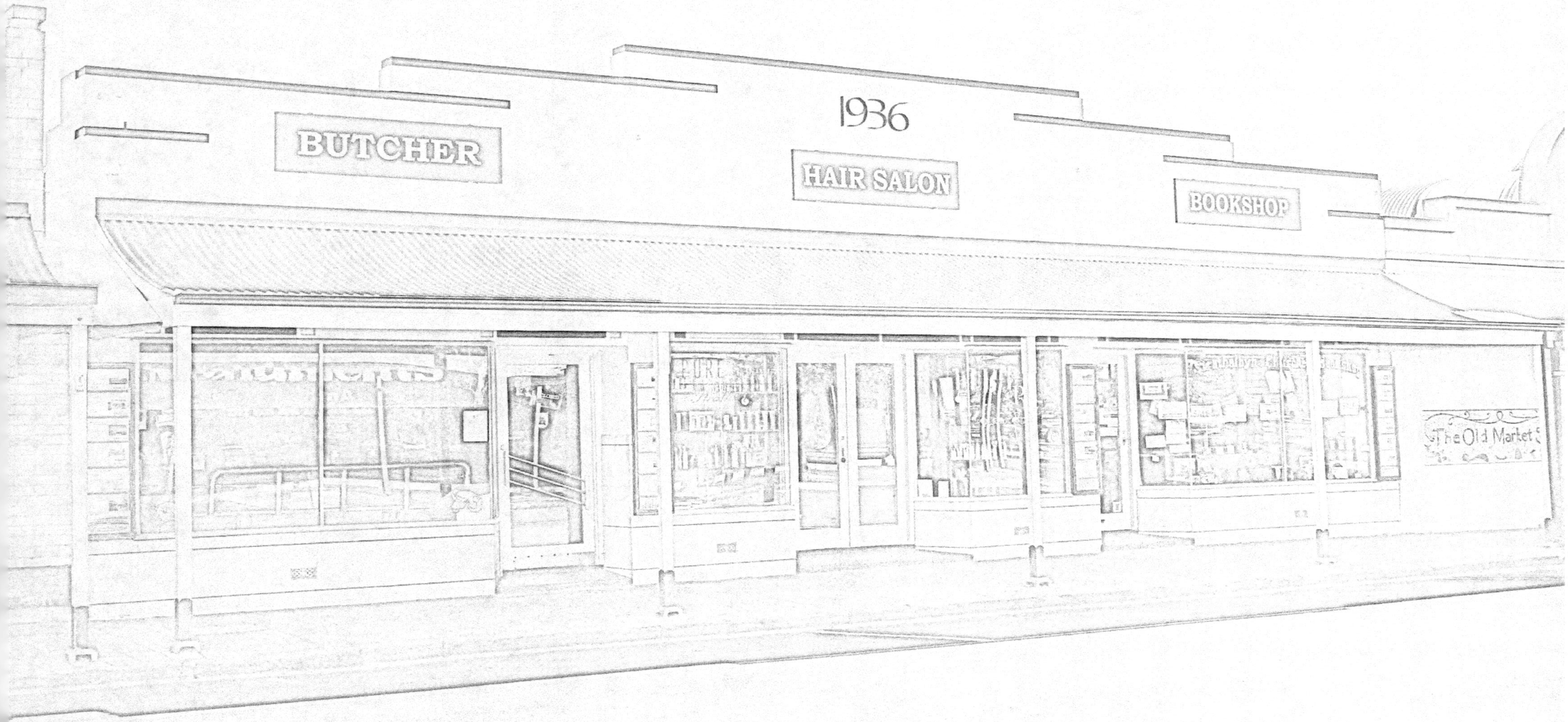
1936
BUTCHER
HAIR SALON
BOOKSHOP

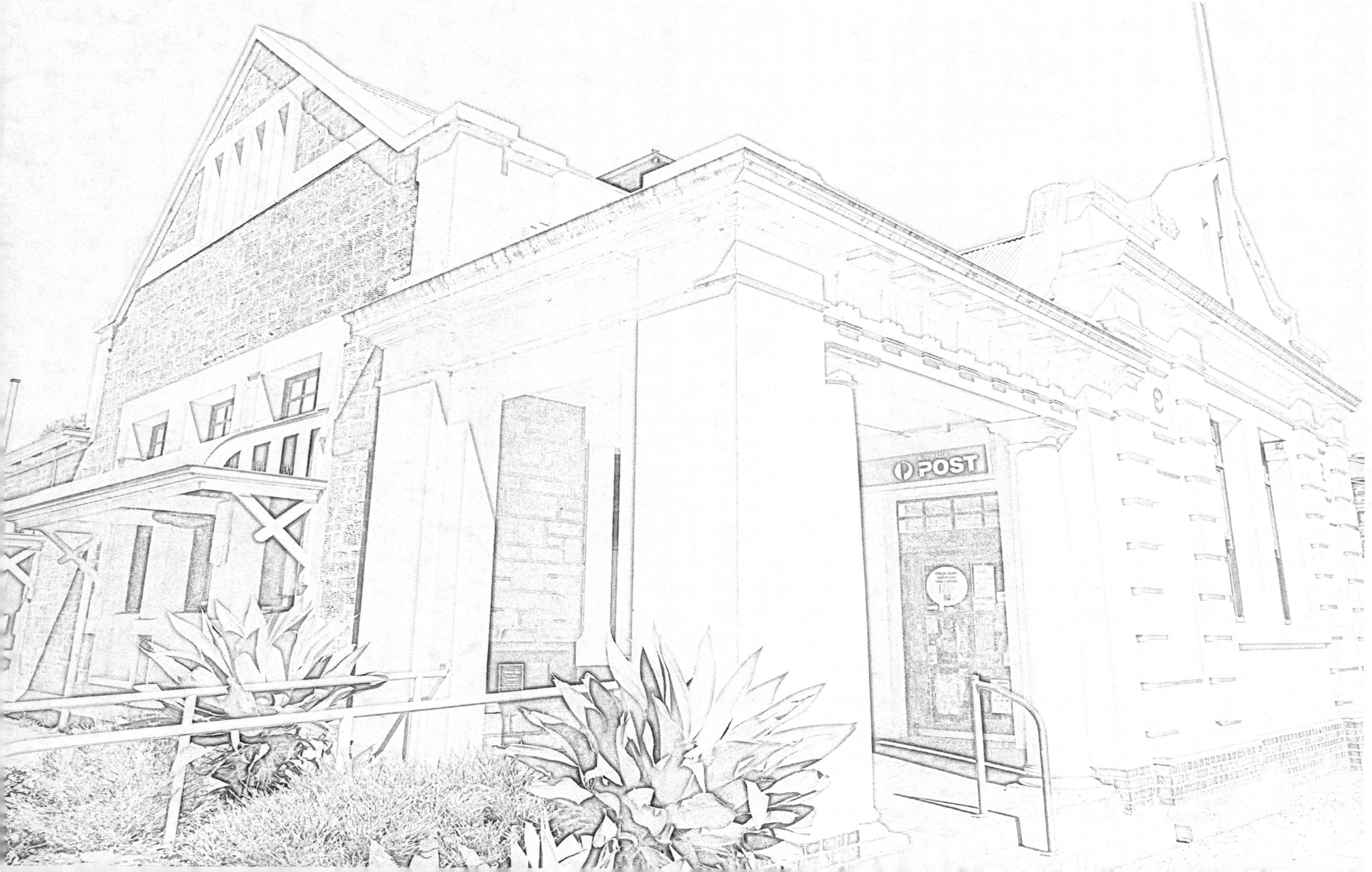
POST

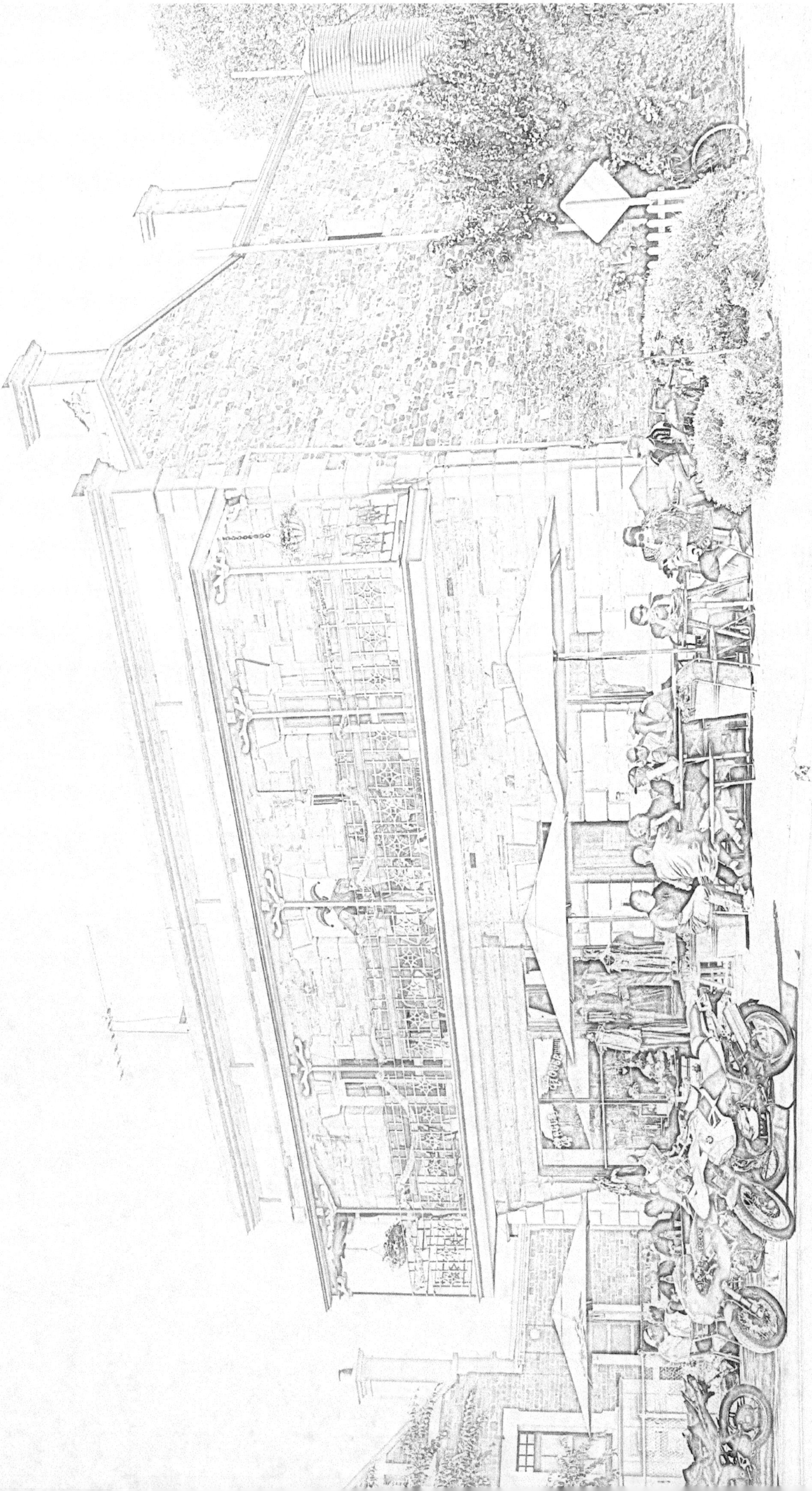

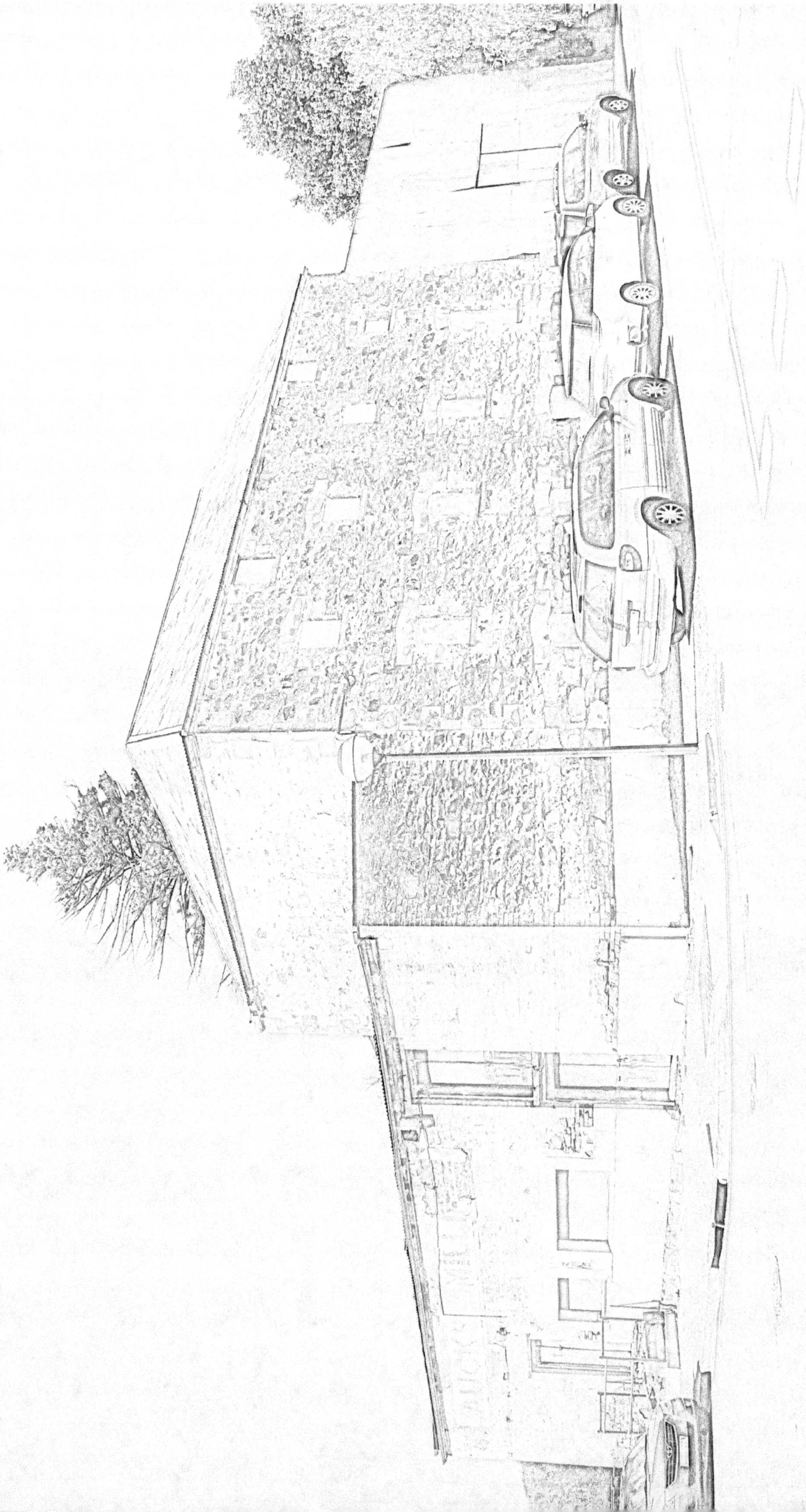

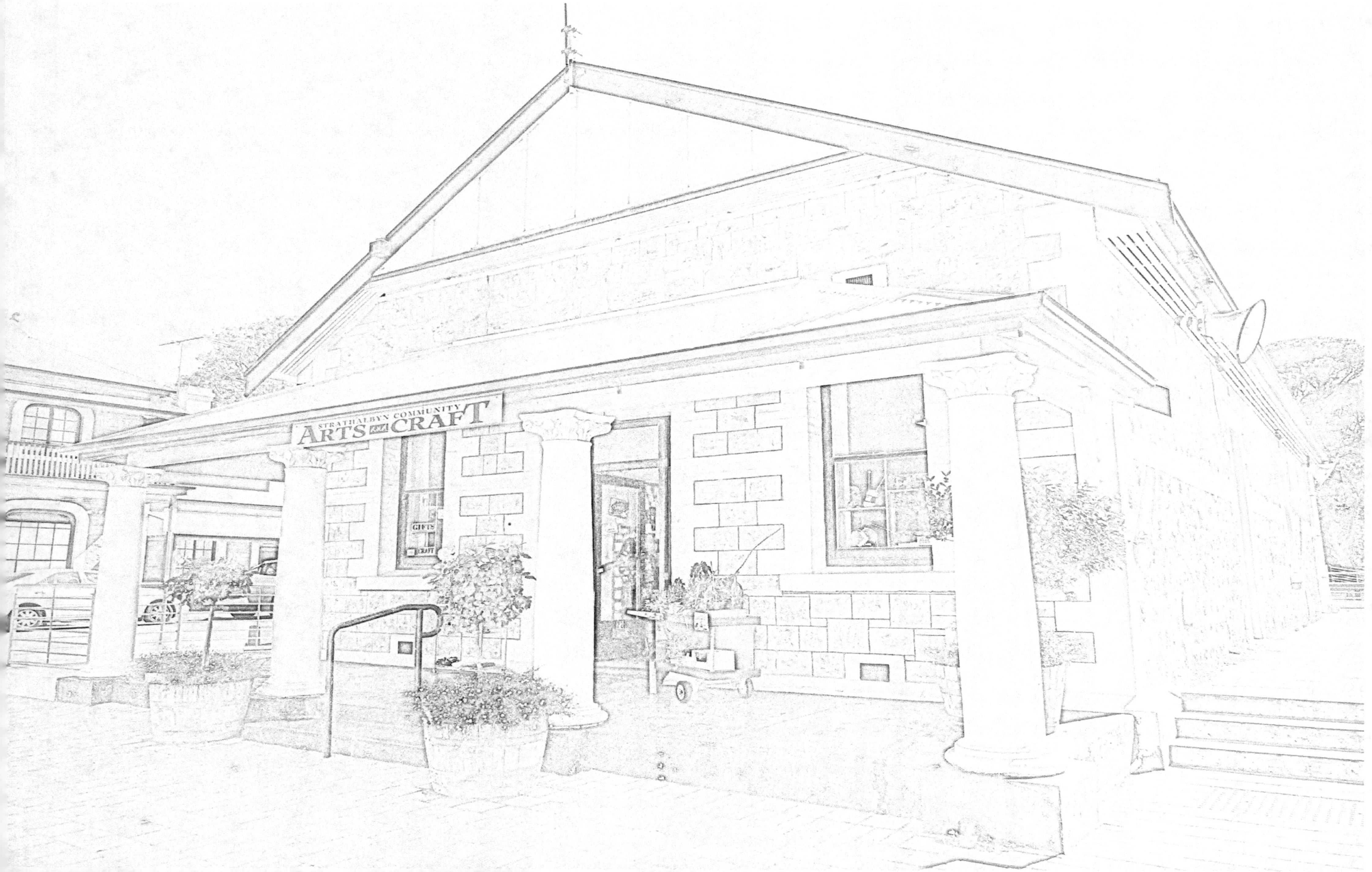
STRATHALBYN COMMUNITY
ARTS and CRAFT
GIFTS

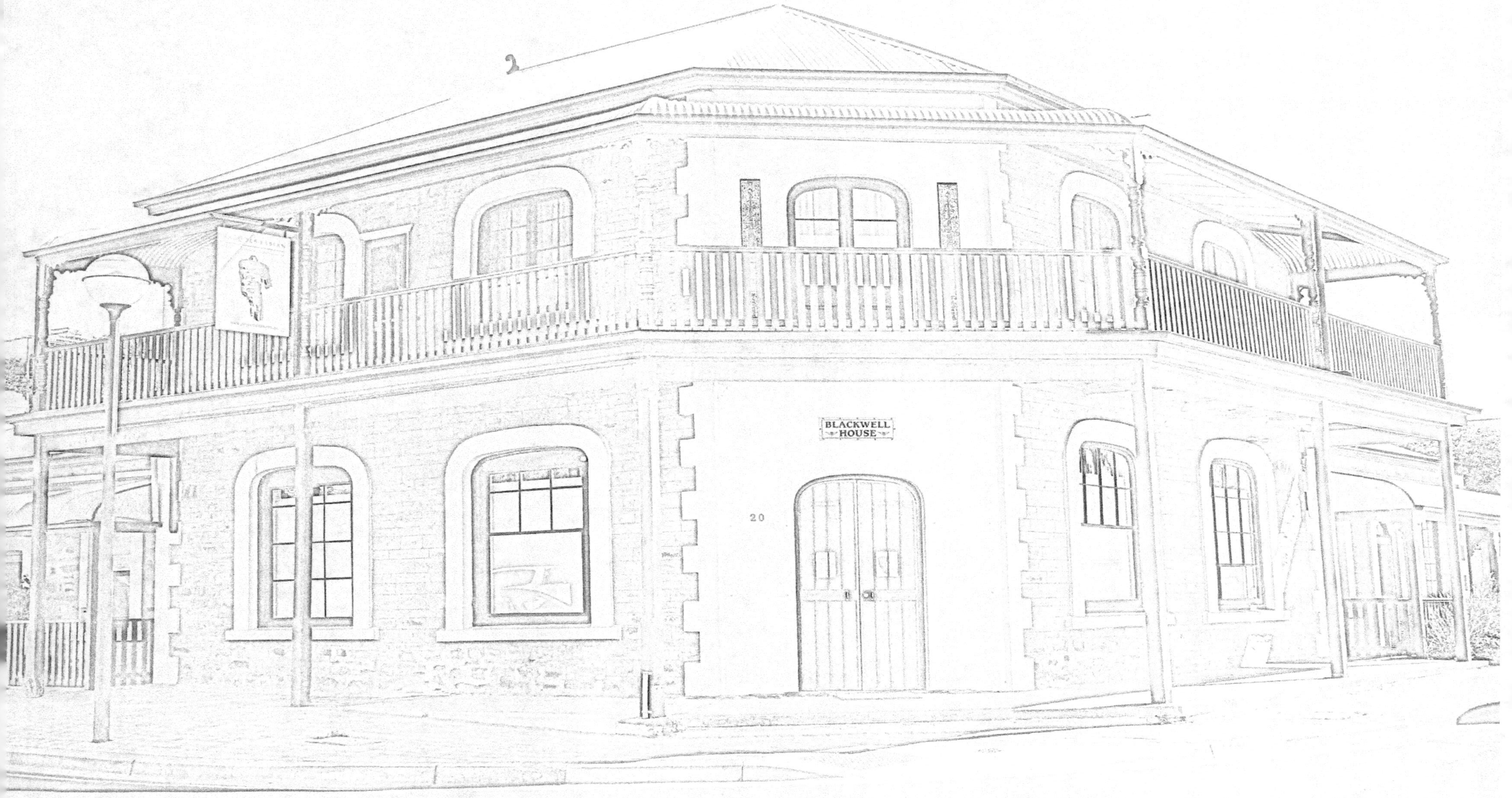
BLACKWELL HOUSE
20

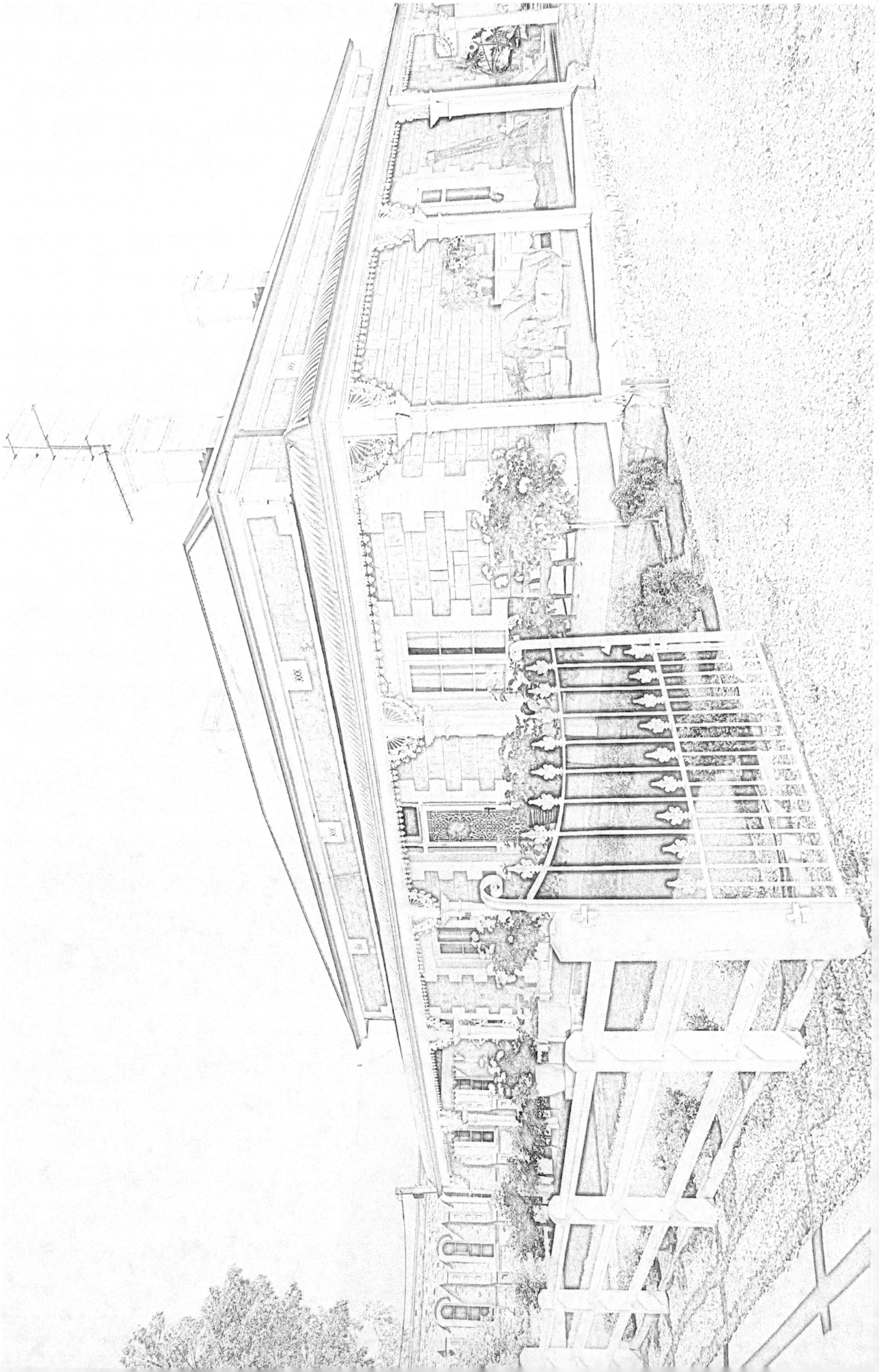

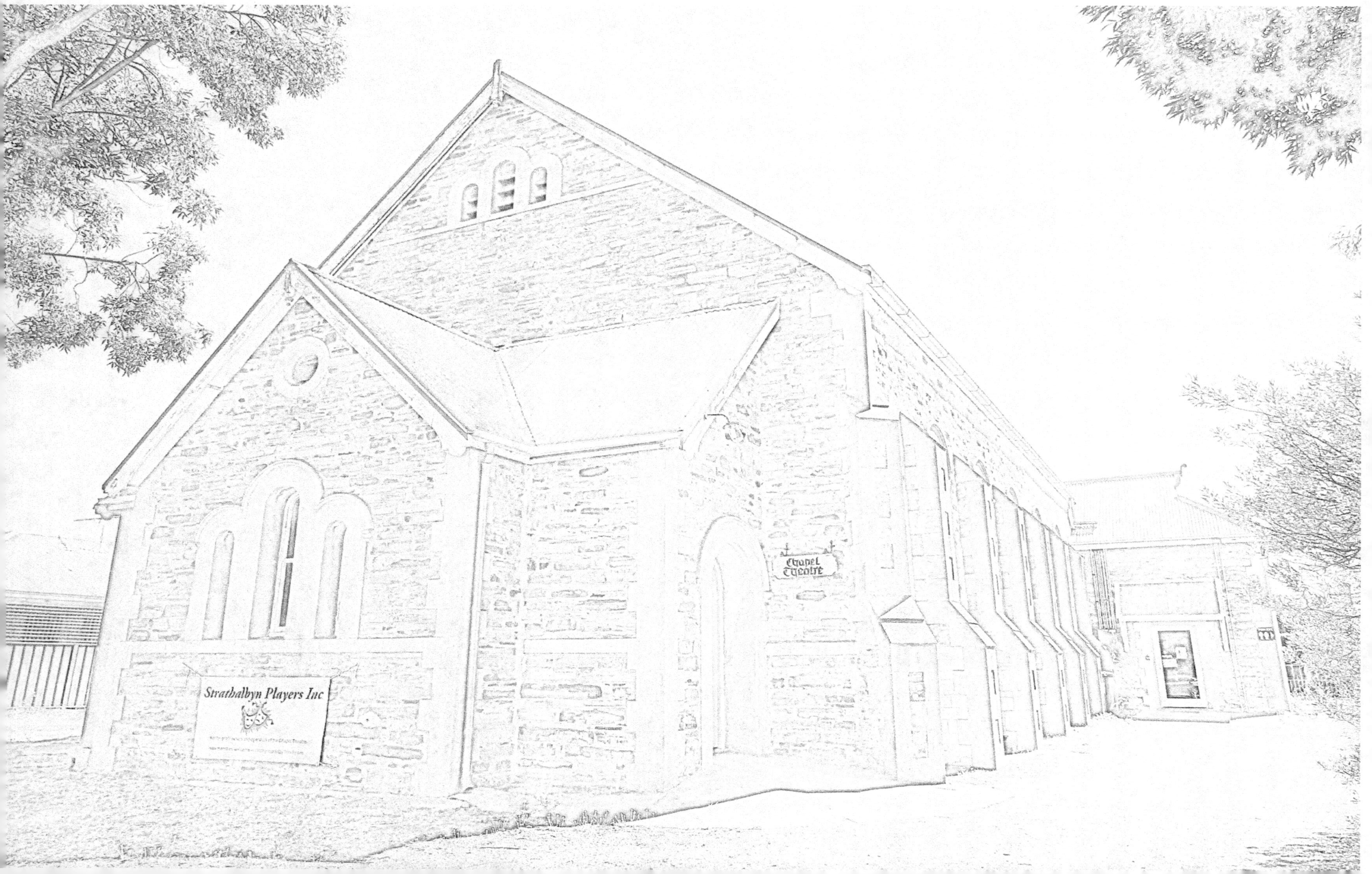

Strathalbyn Players Inc
Chapel Theatre

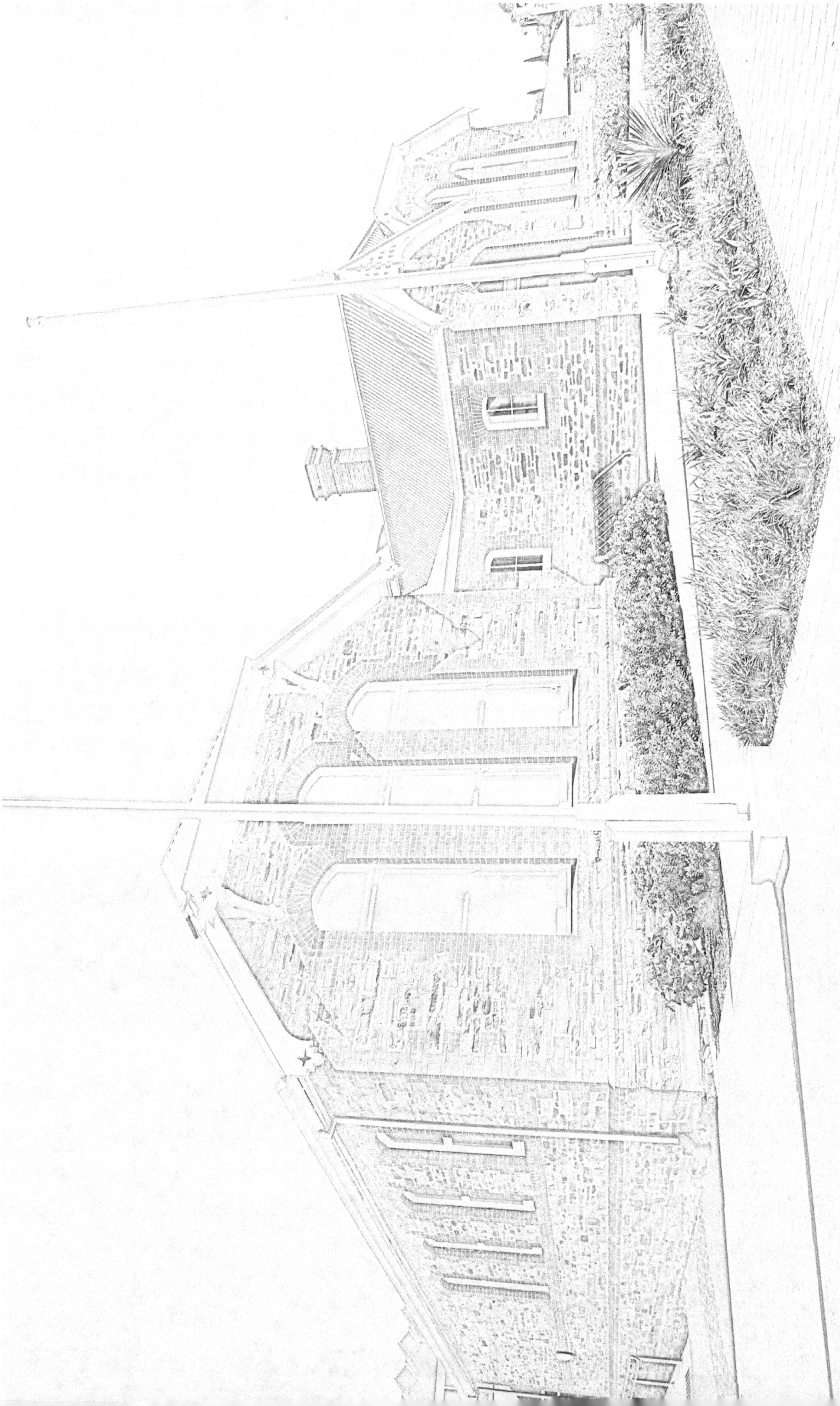

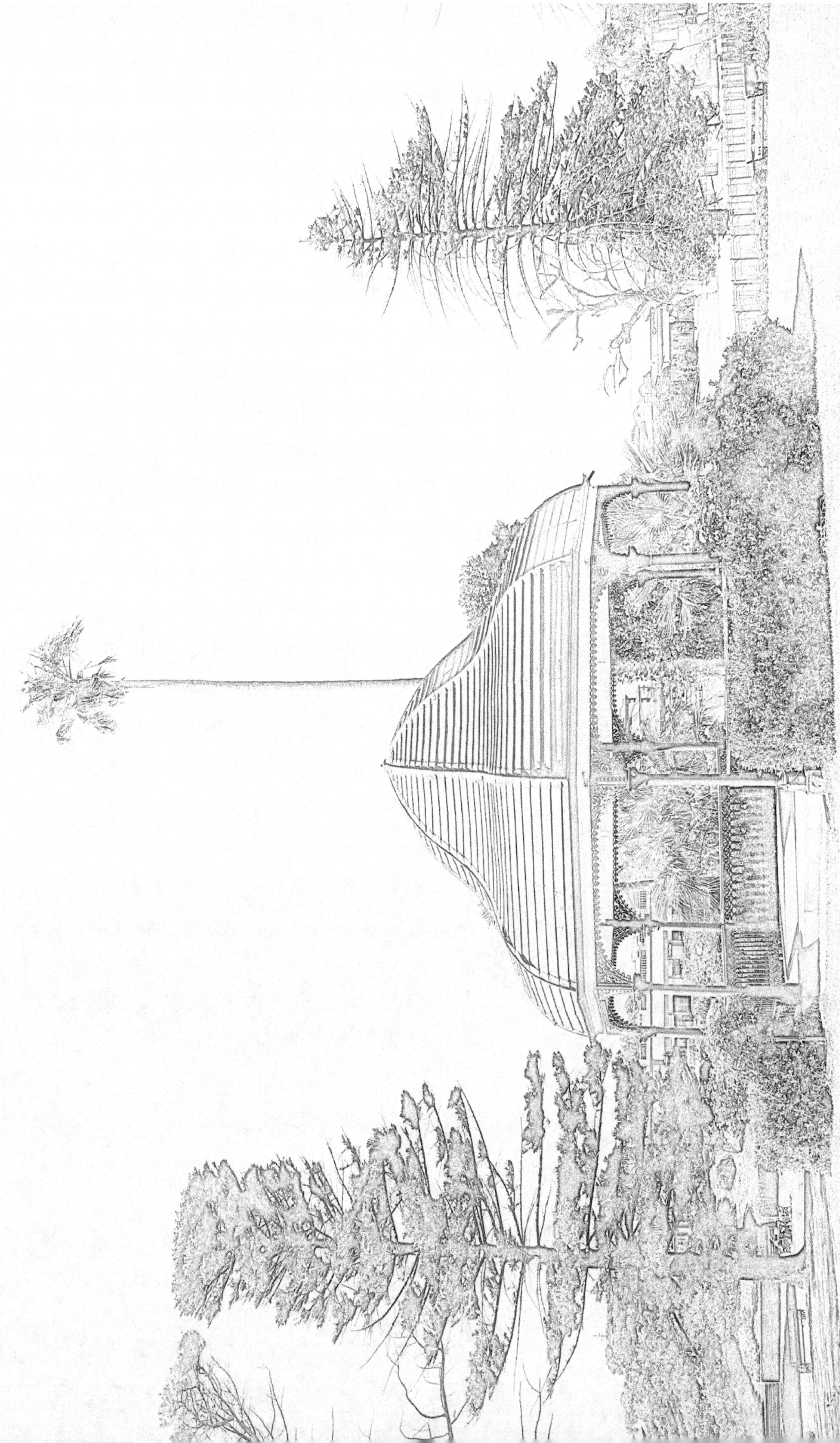

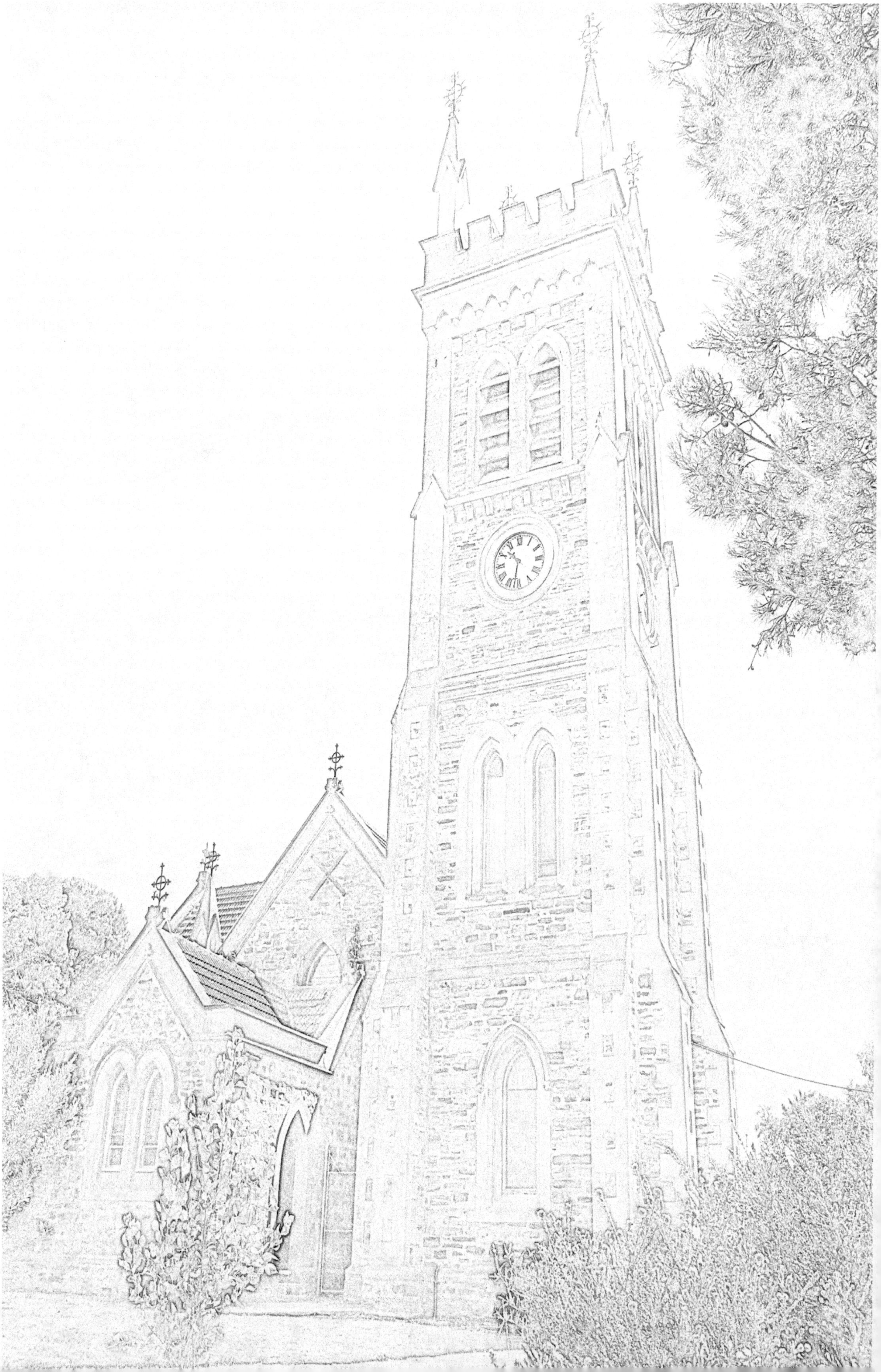

ST. ANDREWS
UNITING CHURCH HALL

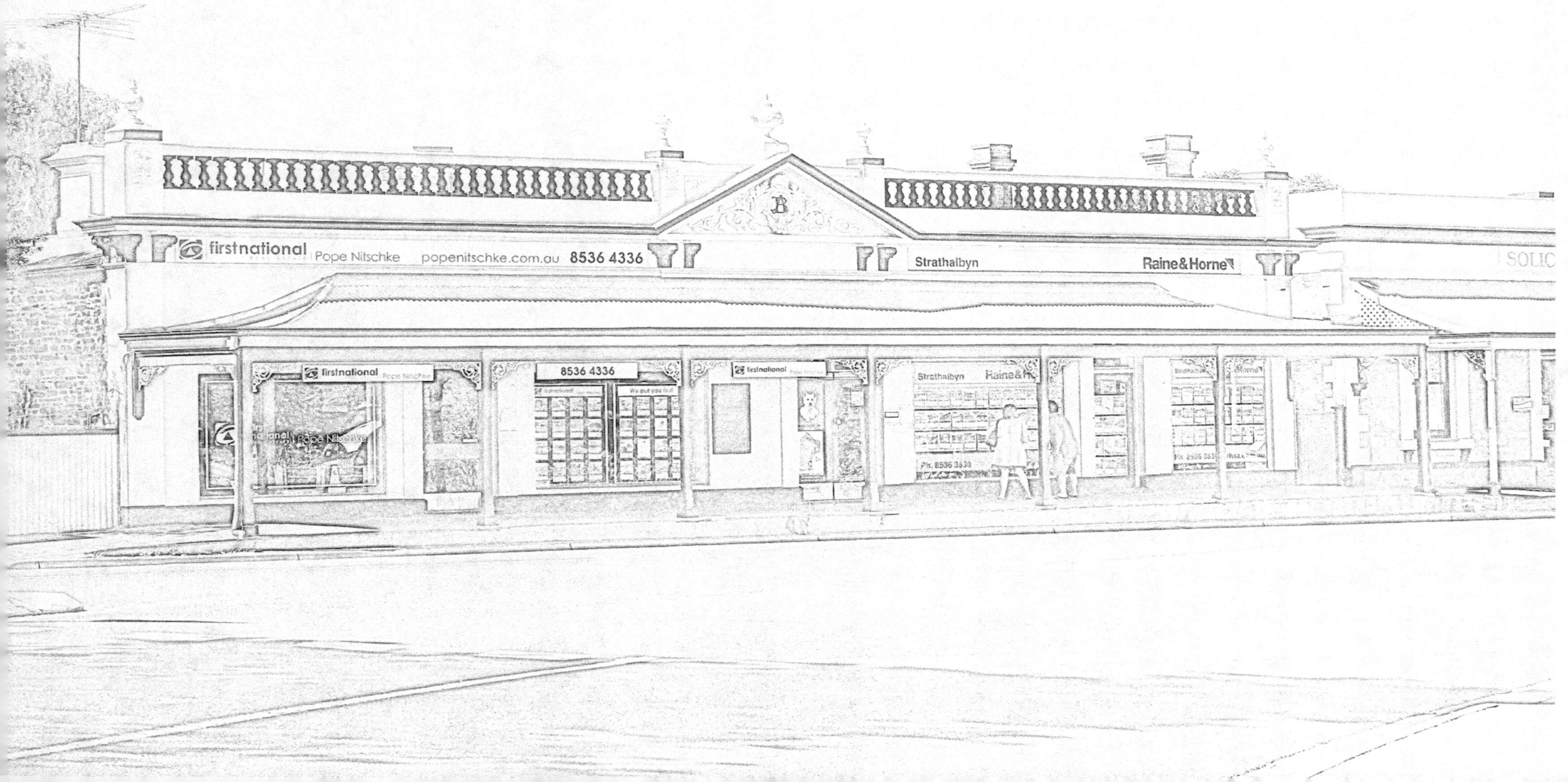
firstnational
Pope Nitschke
popenitschke.com.au
8536 4336
Strathalbyn
Raine&Horne
8536 4336
We put you first
Ph. 8536 3330

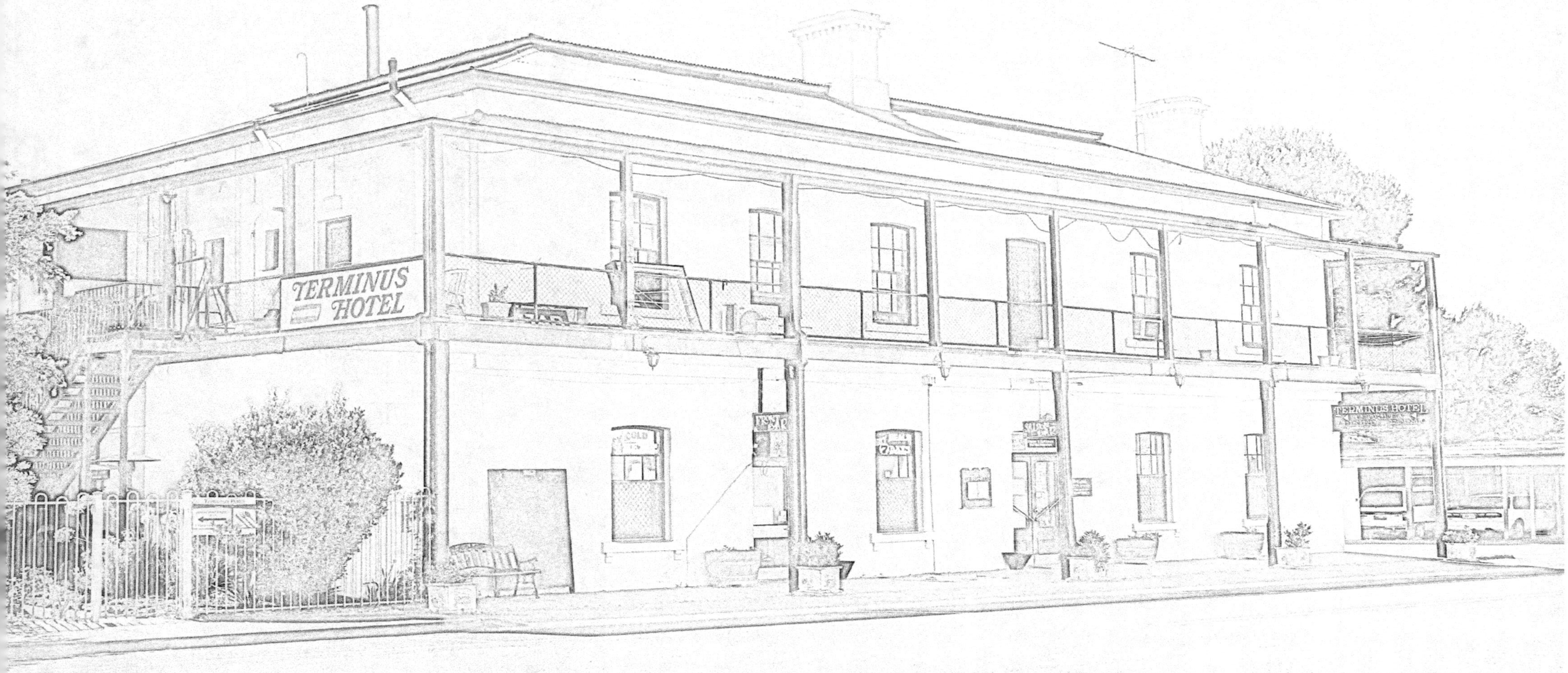
TERMINUS HOTEL
TERMINUS HOTEL

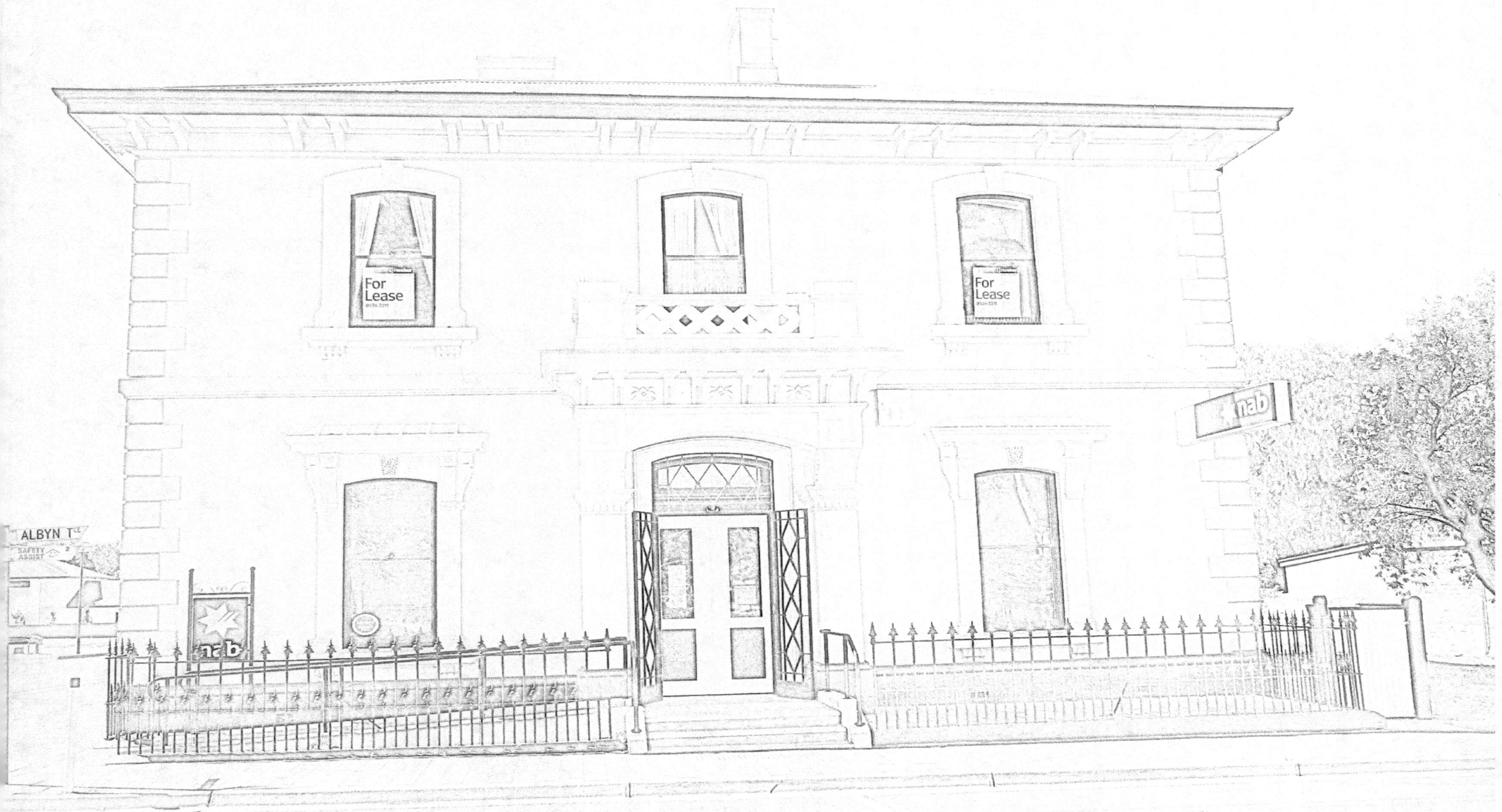
For Lease
For Lease
nab
nab
ALBYN T^CE
SAFETY ASSIST

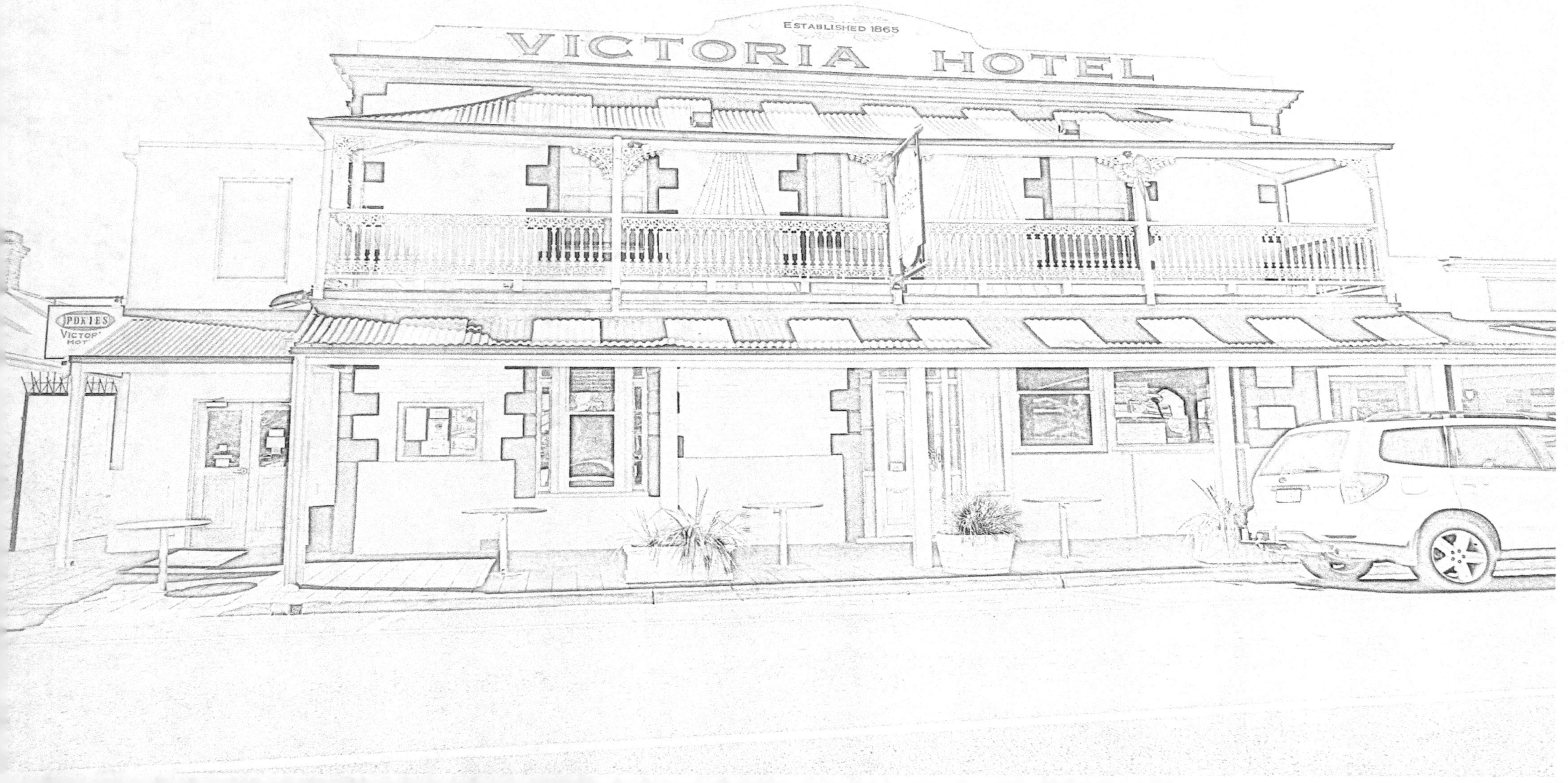
ESTABLISHED 1865
VICTORIA HOTEL
POKIES
VICTOR
HOT

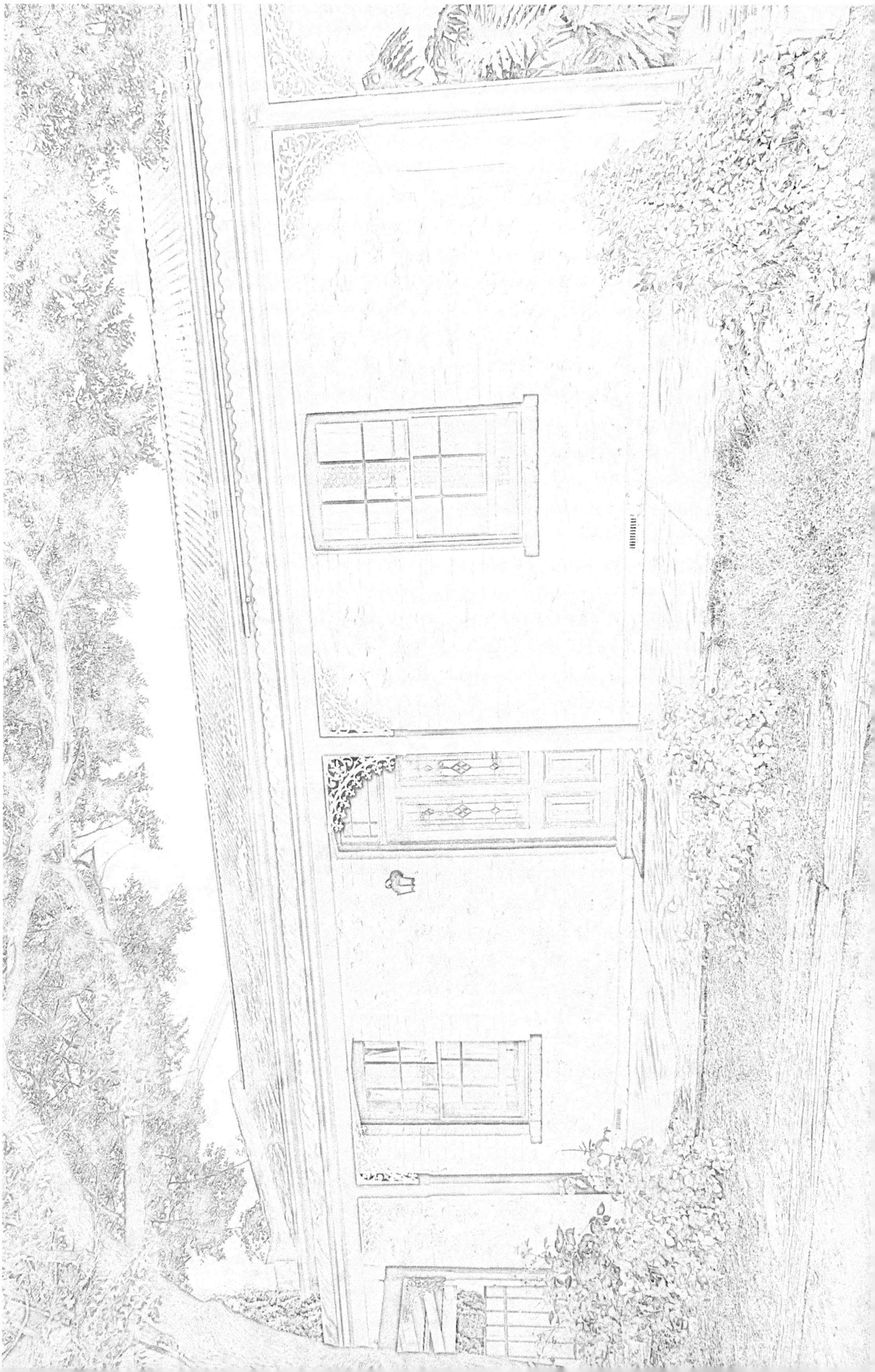

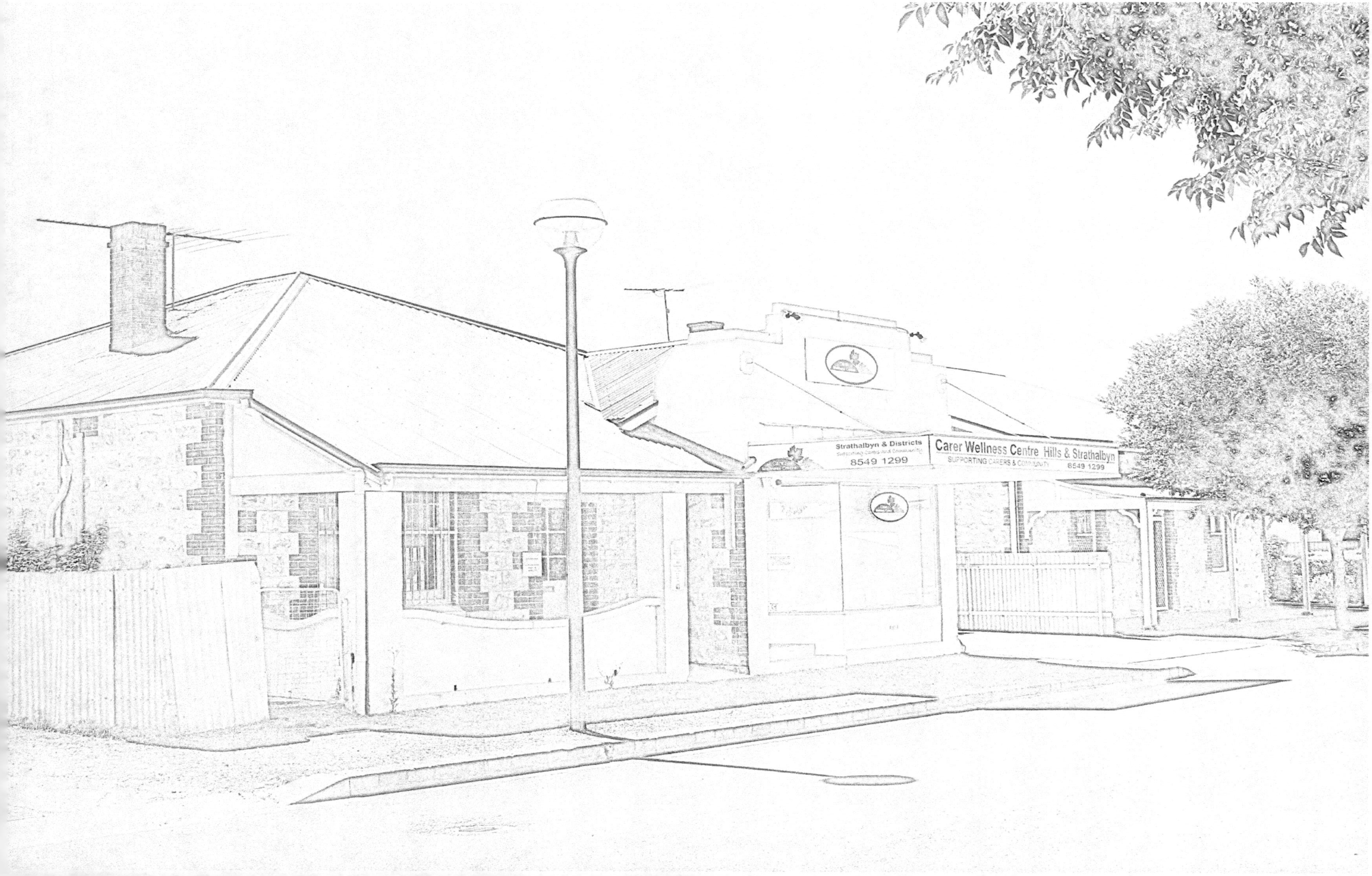
Strathalbyn & Districts
8549 1299
Carer Wellness Centre Hills & Strathalbyn
SUPPORTING CARERS & COMMUNITY
8549 1299

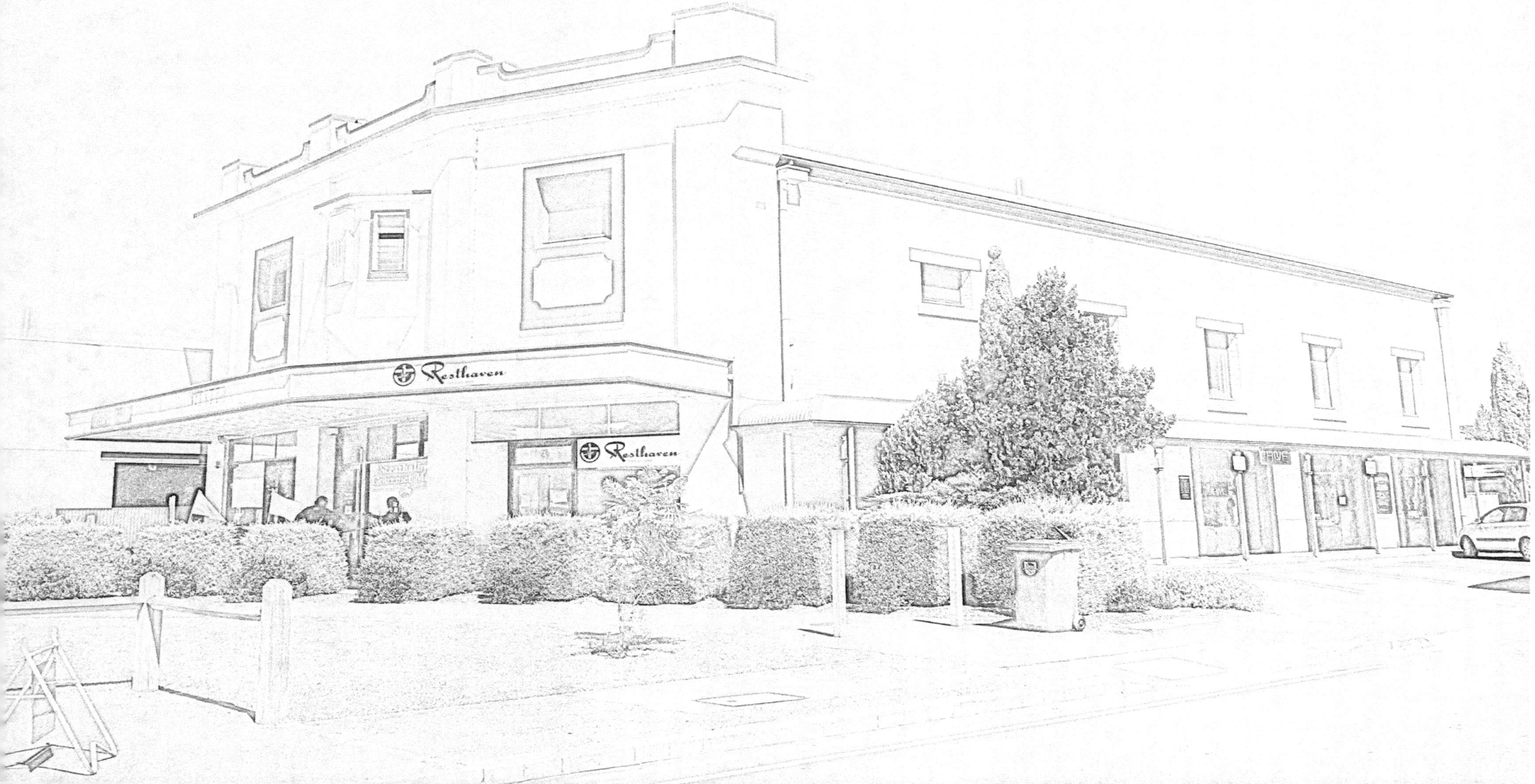
Resthaven
Resthaven

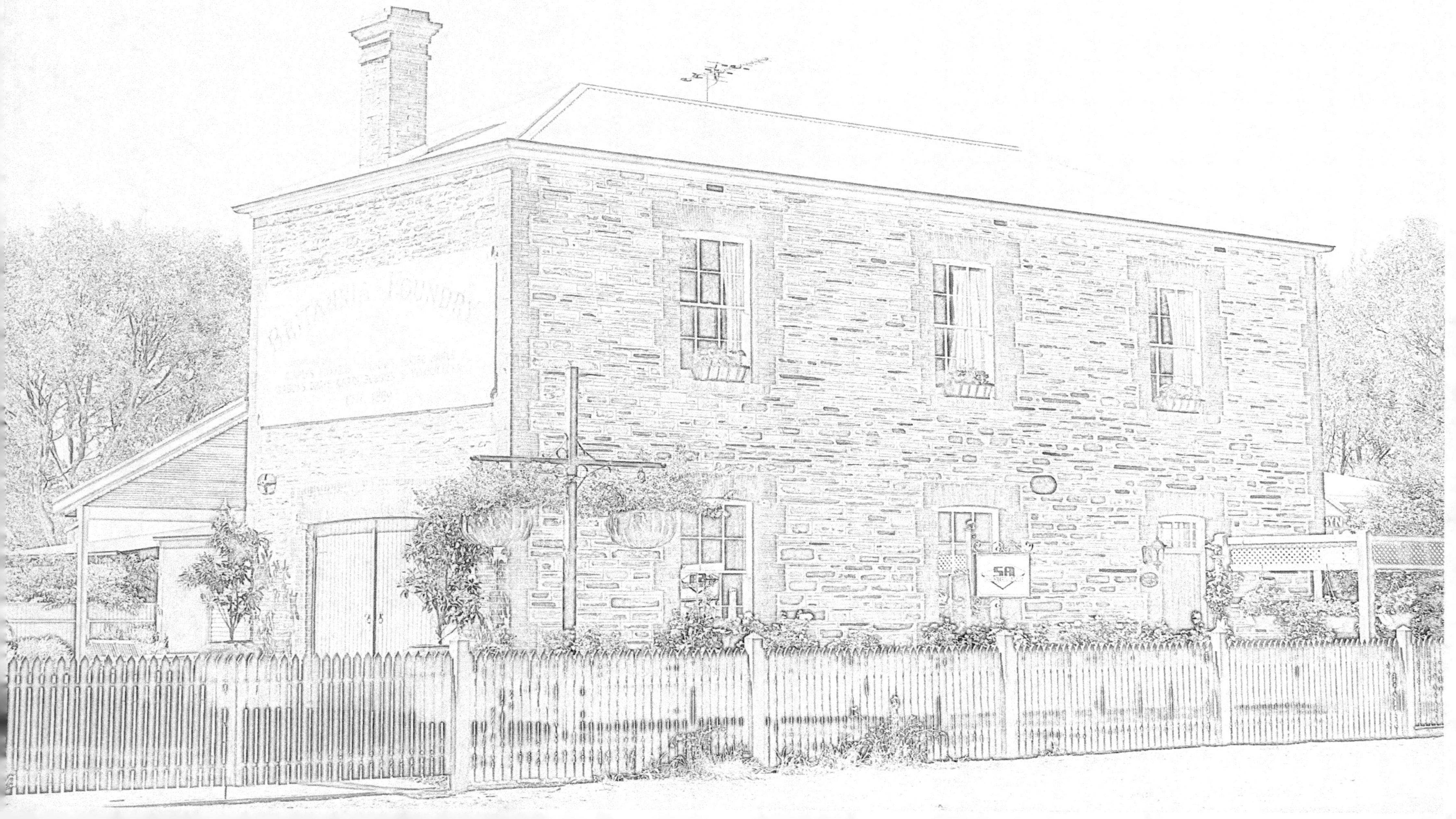

CHICKEN PIZZA FISH & CHIPS
DINE IN TAKE AWAY
Pizza Chicken
FISH & CHIPS
PIZZA
CHICKEN
COIN OP LAUNDRY
All Beef. No bull.
AMICI

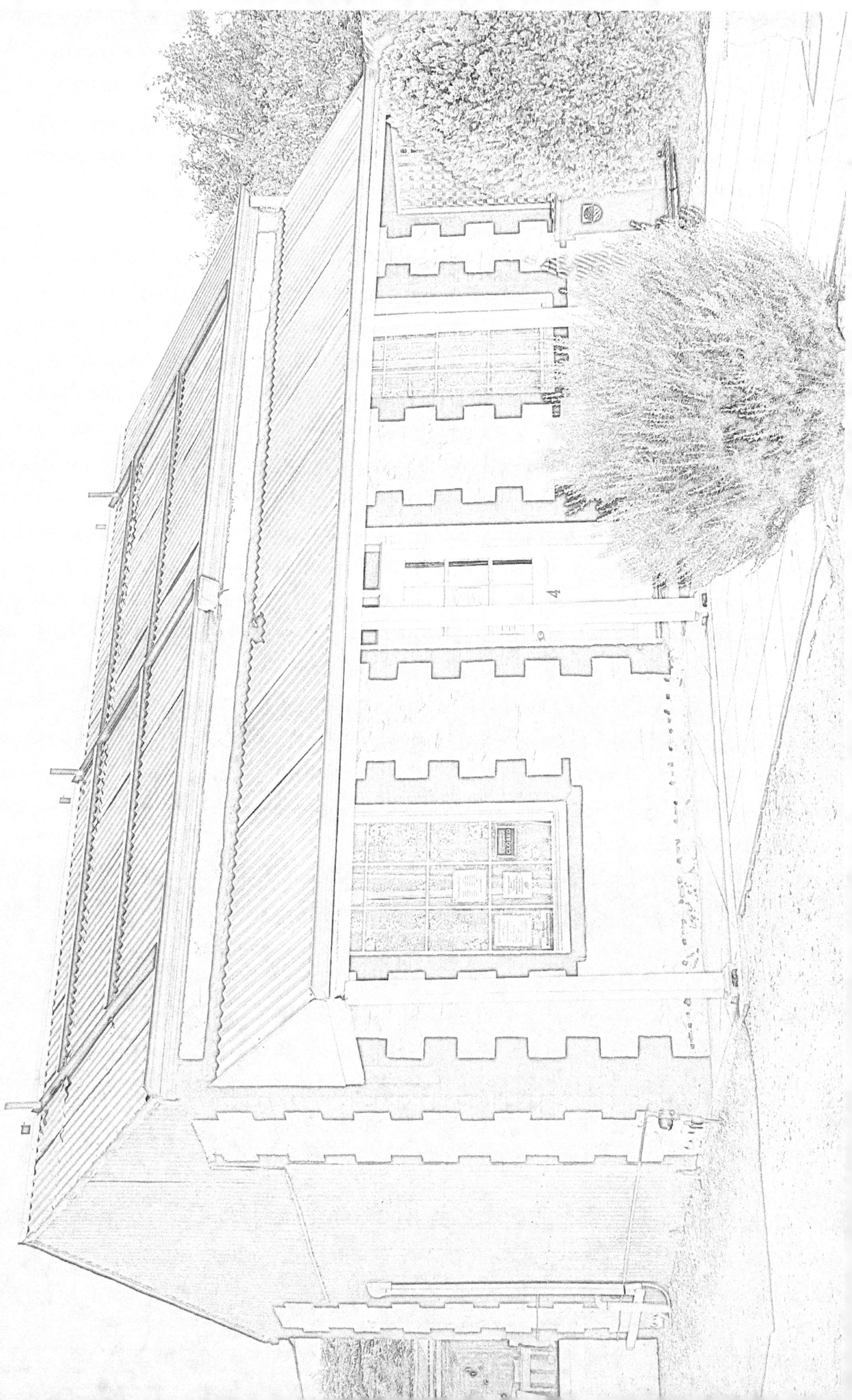

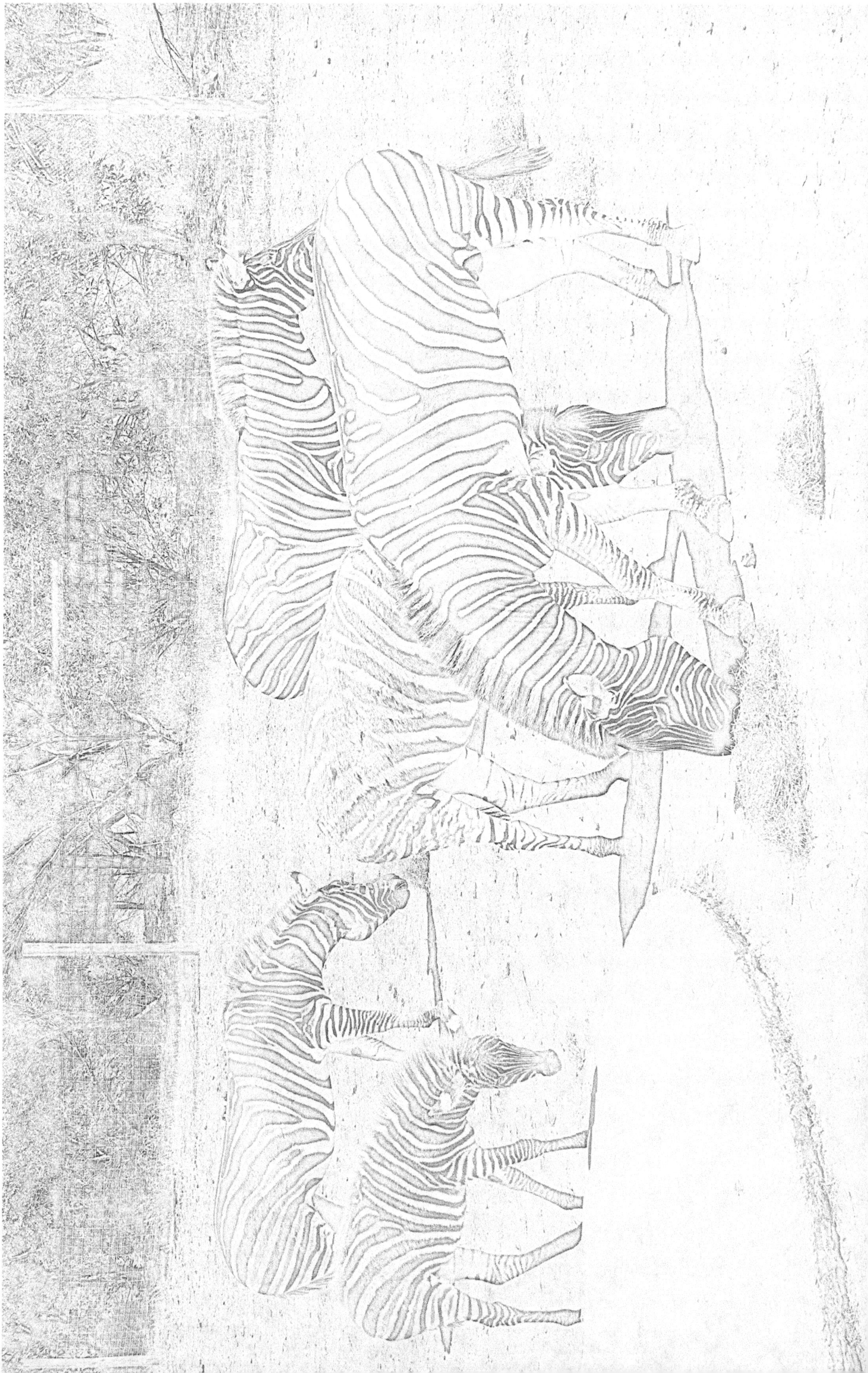

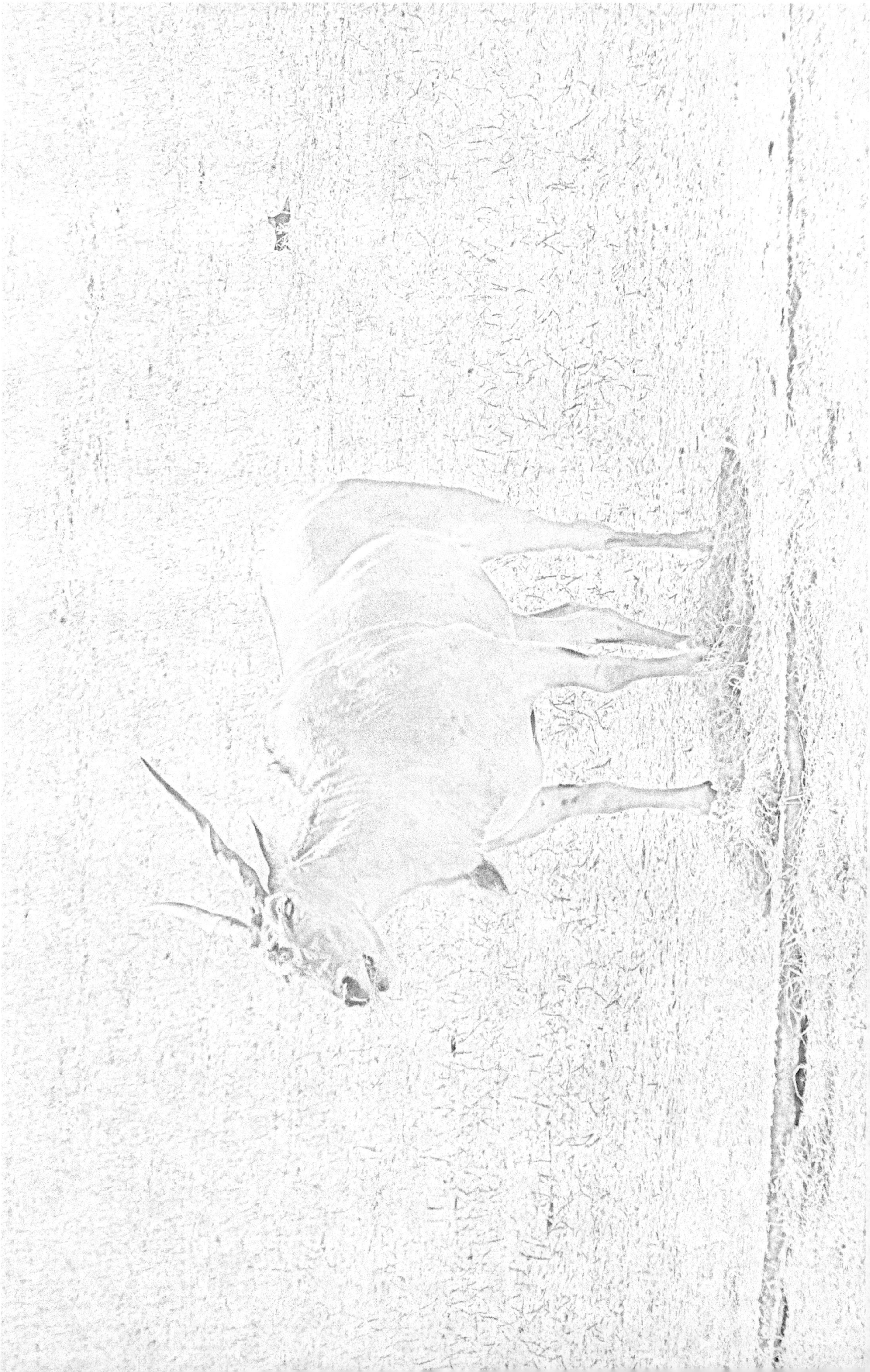

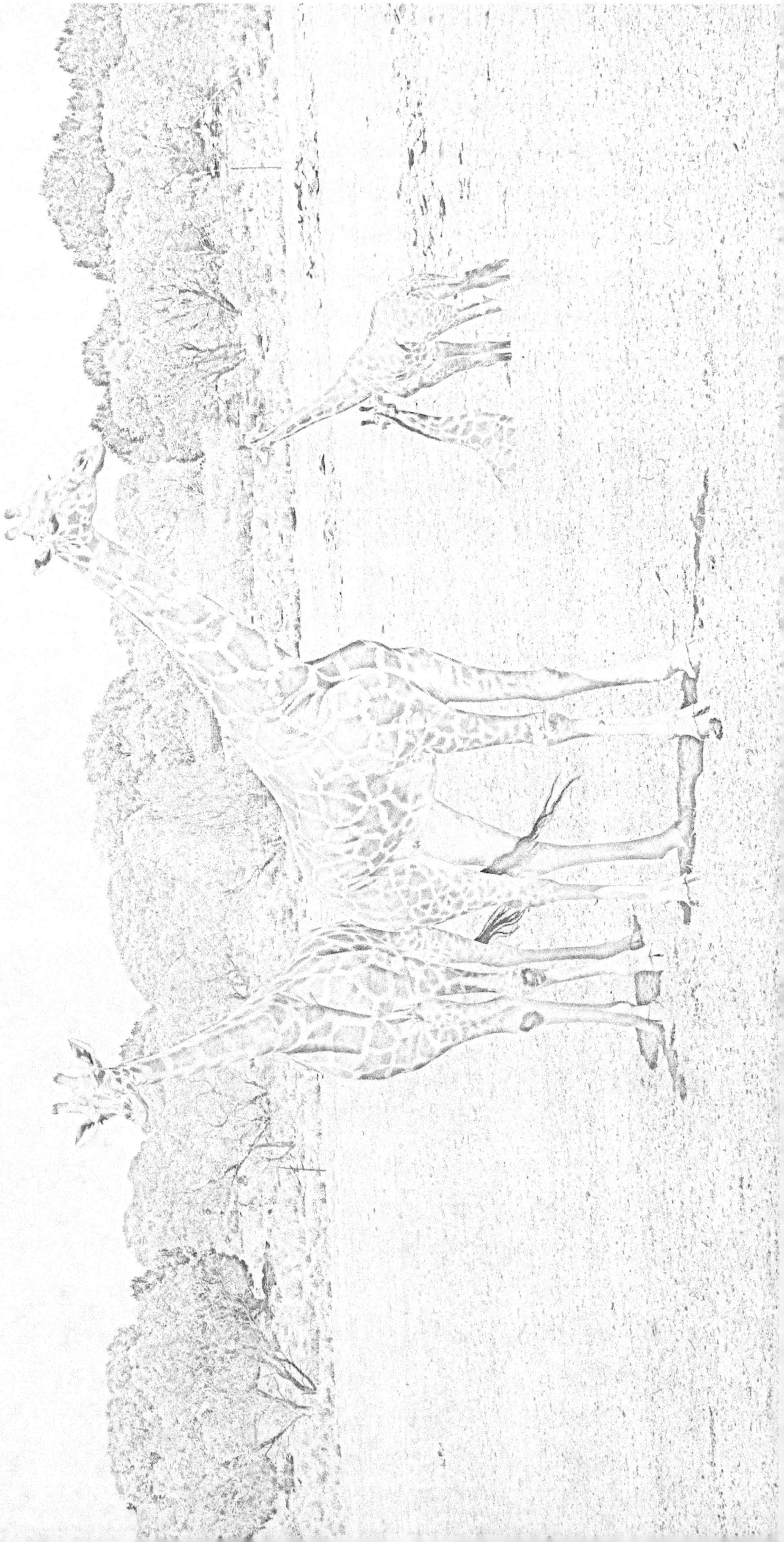

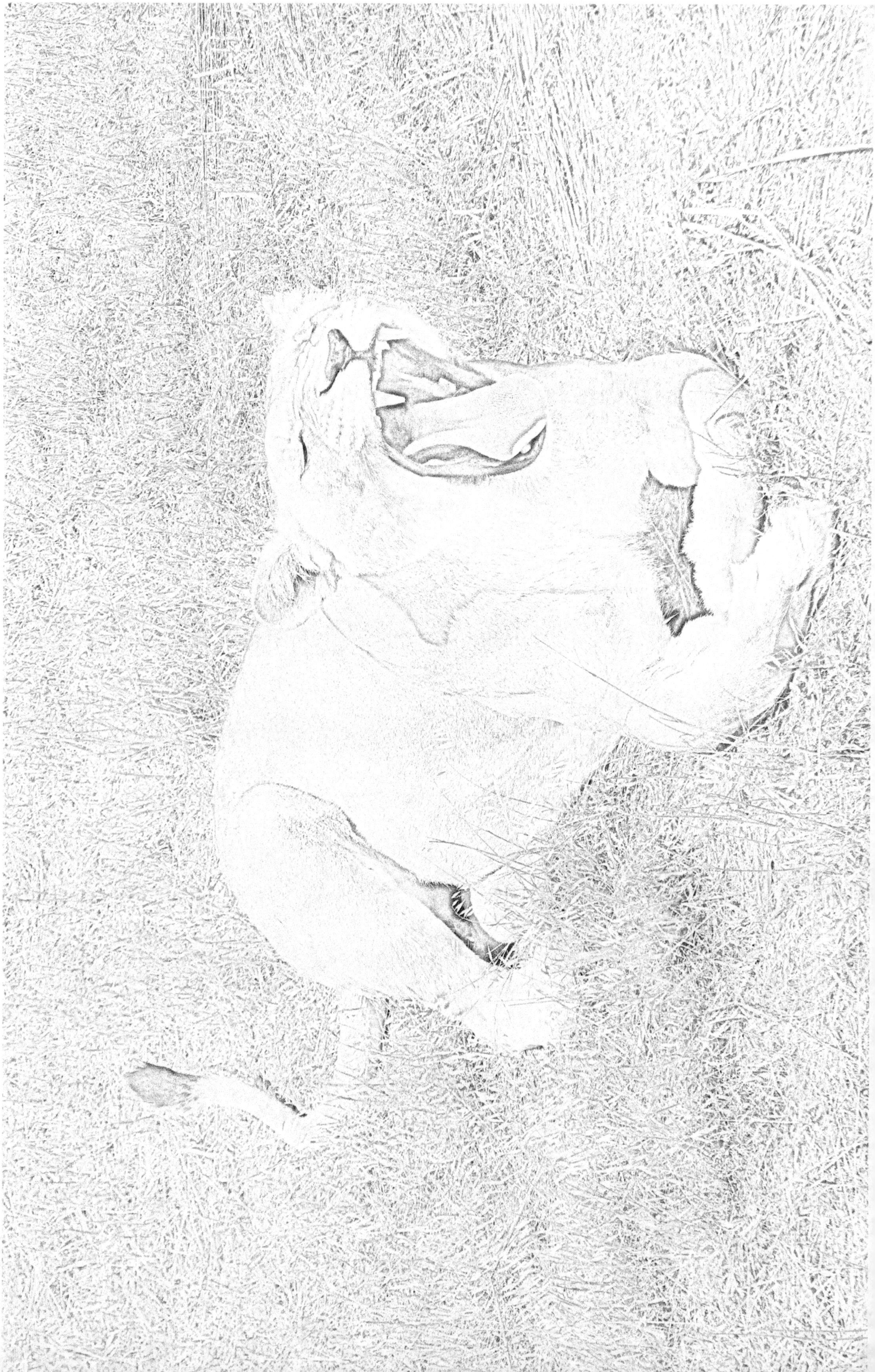

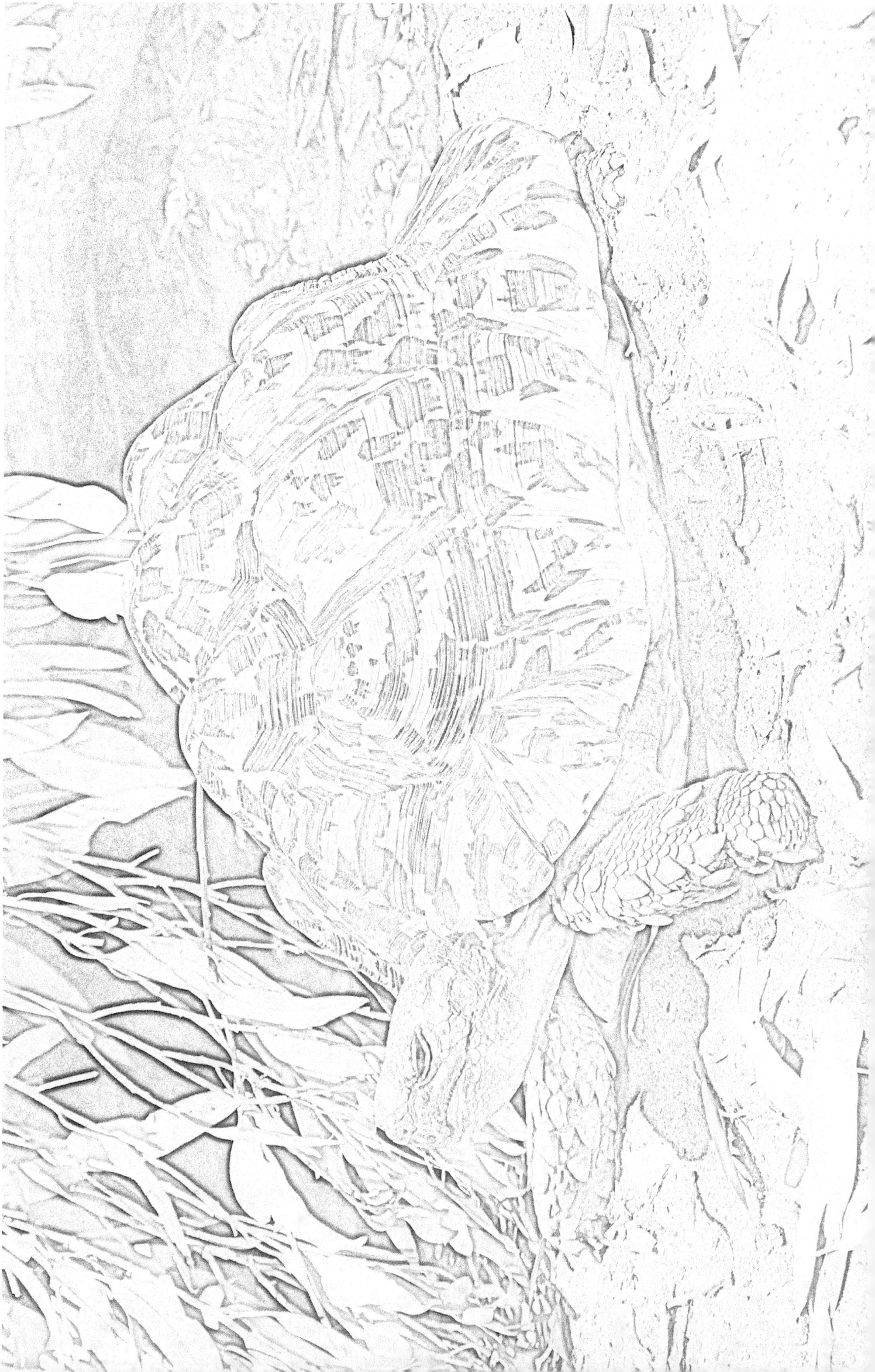

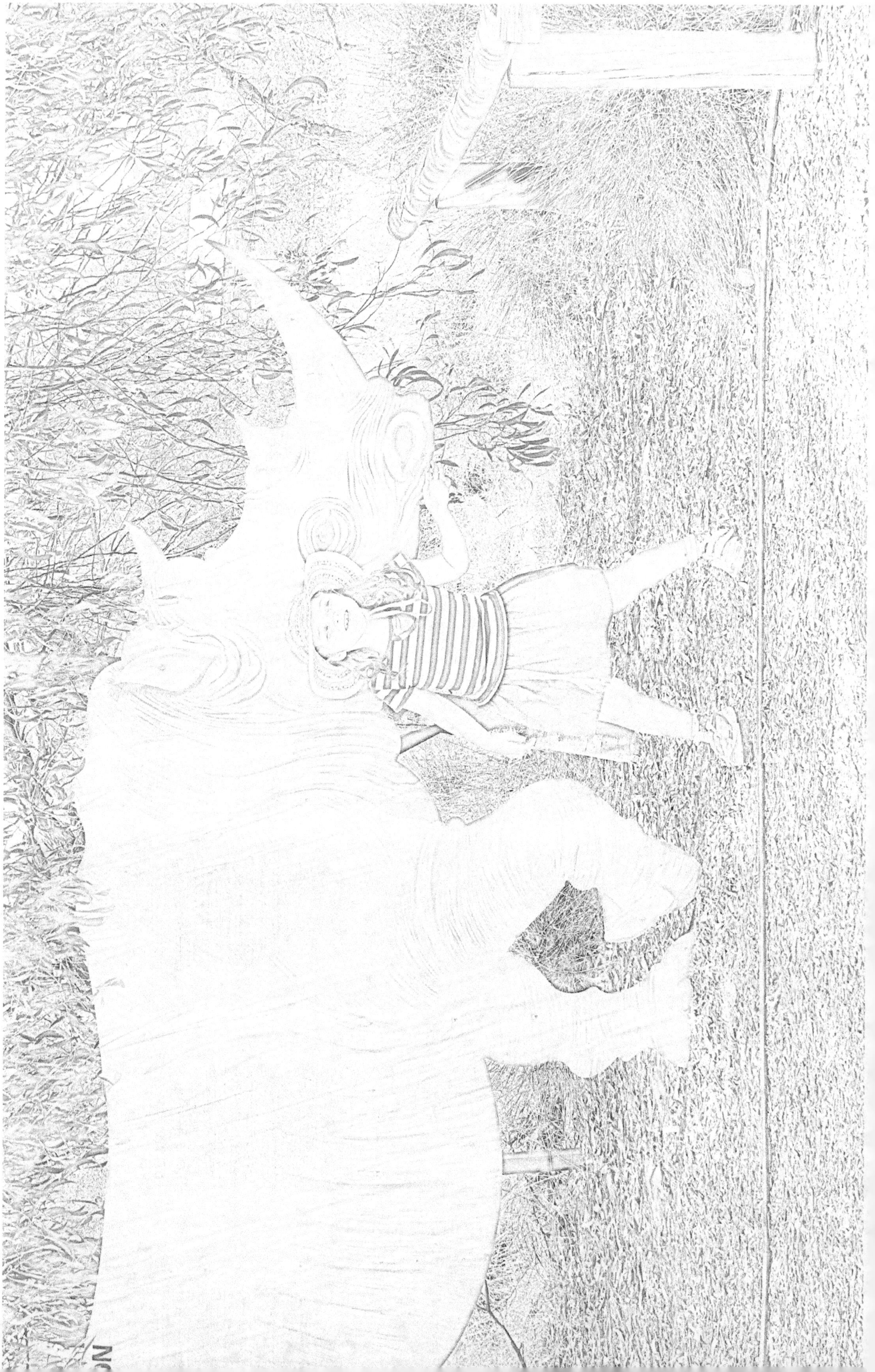

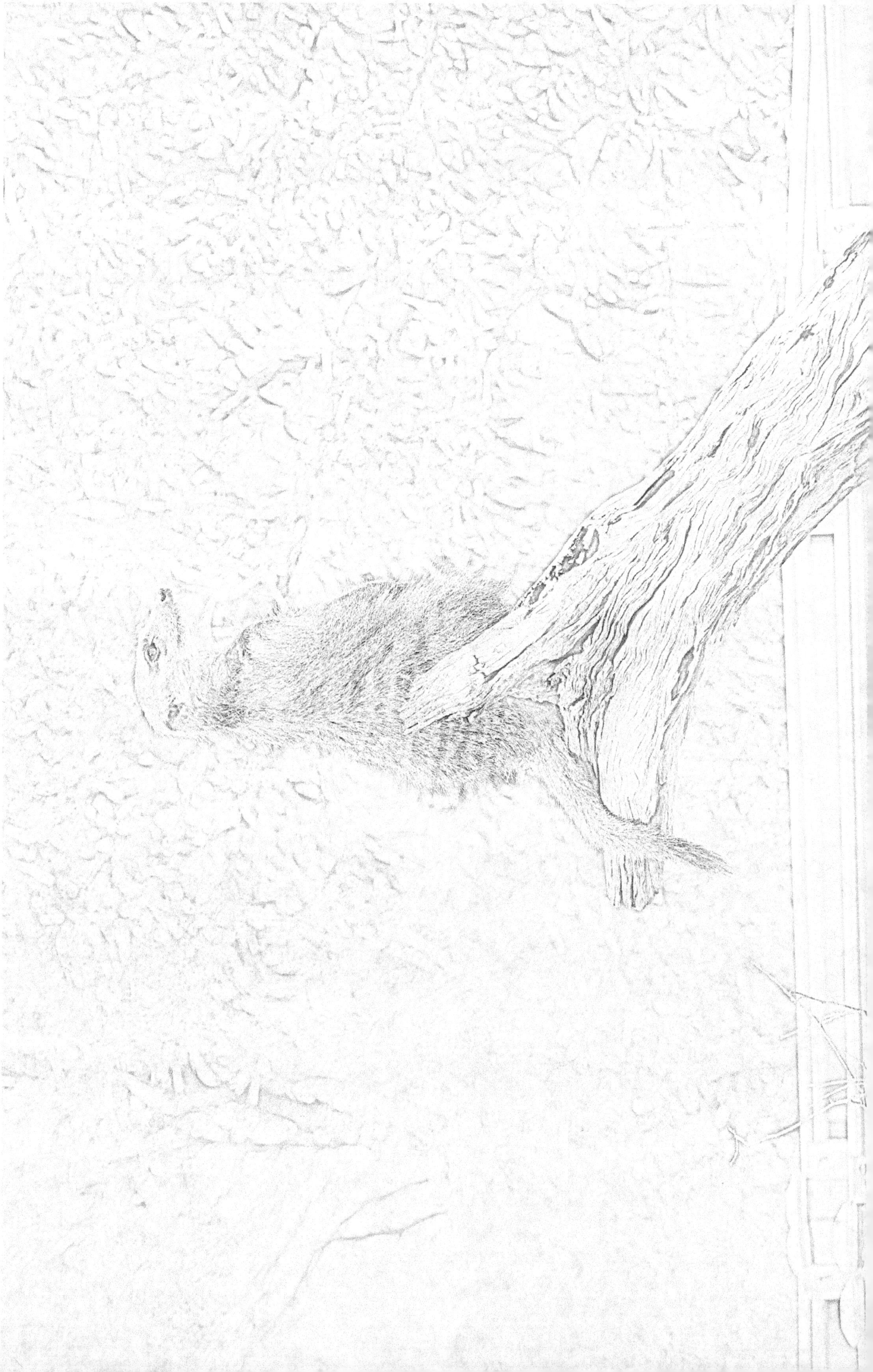

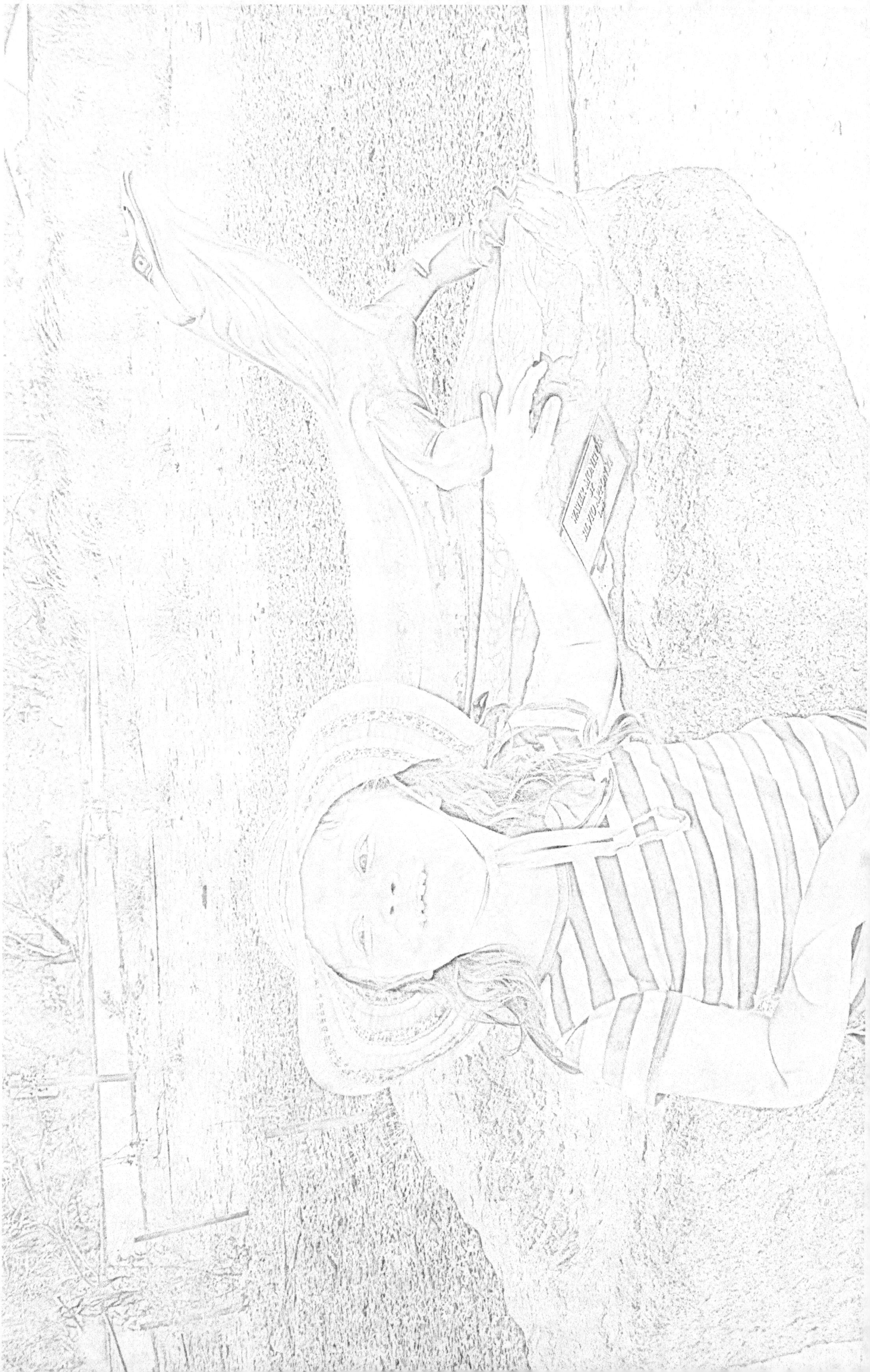

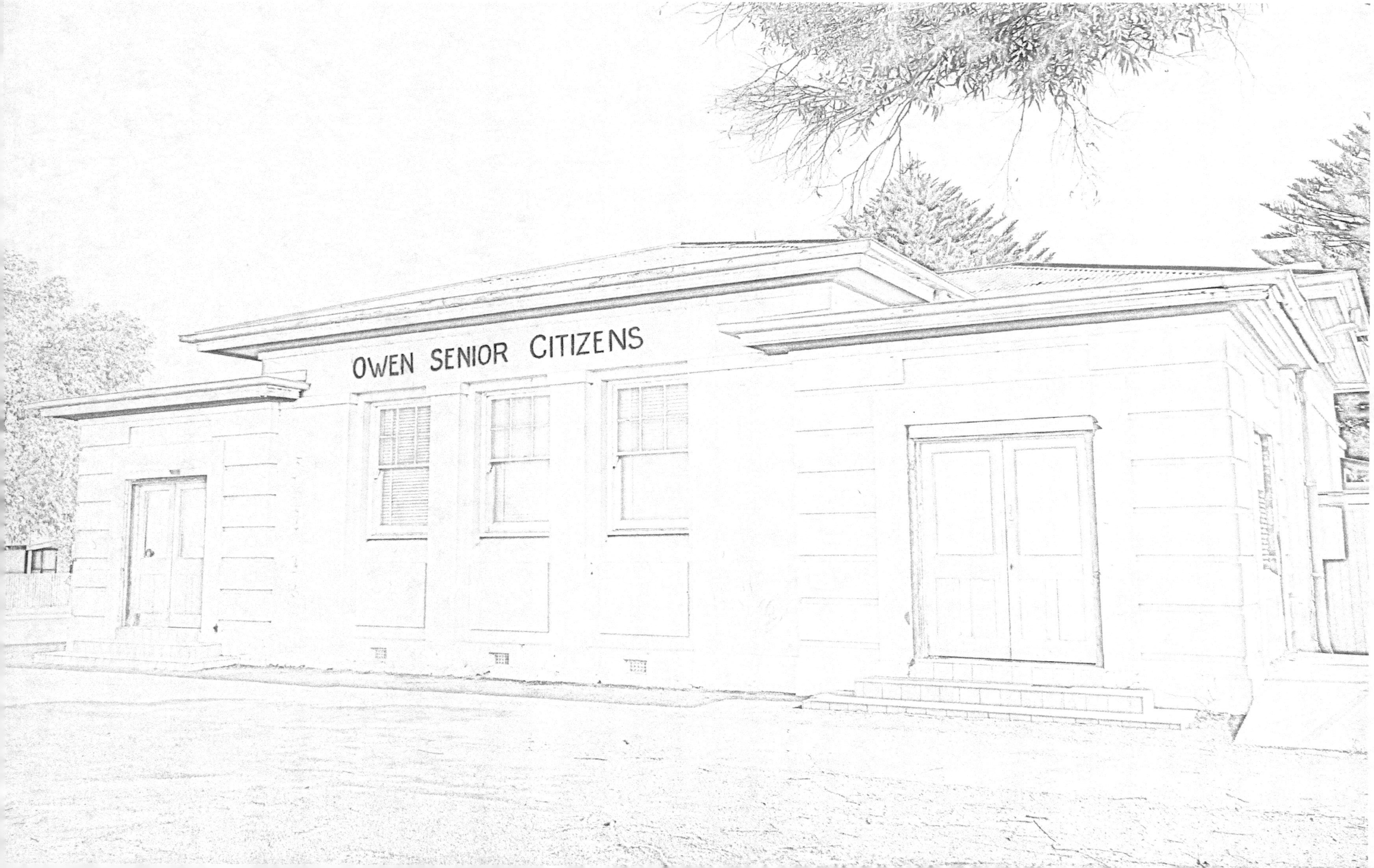
OWEN SENIOR CITIZENS

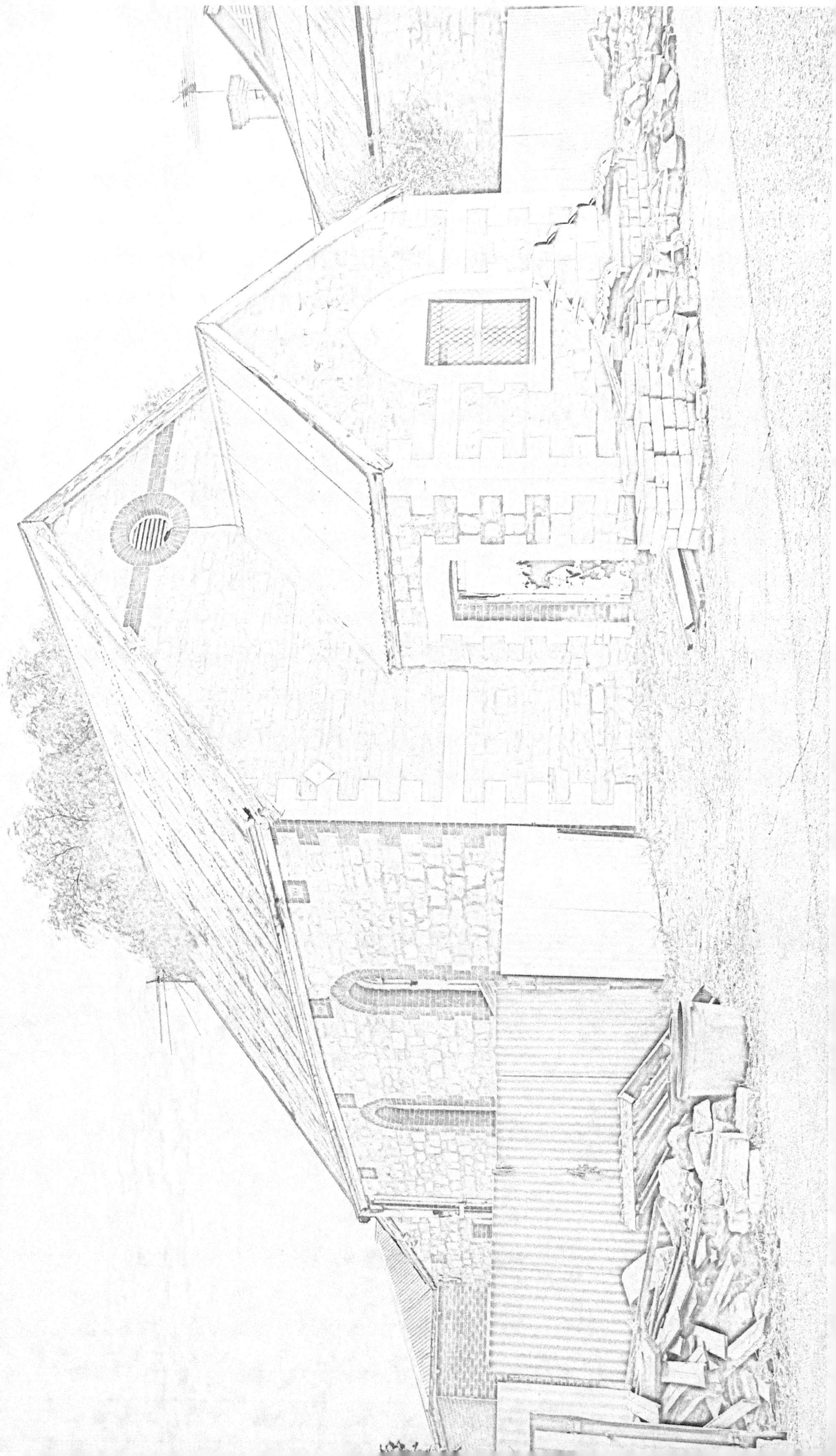

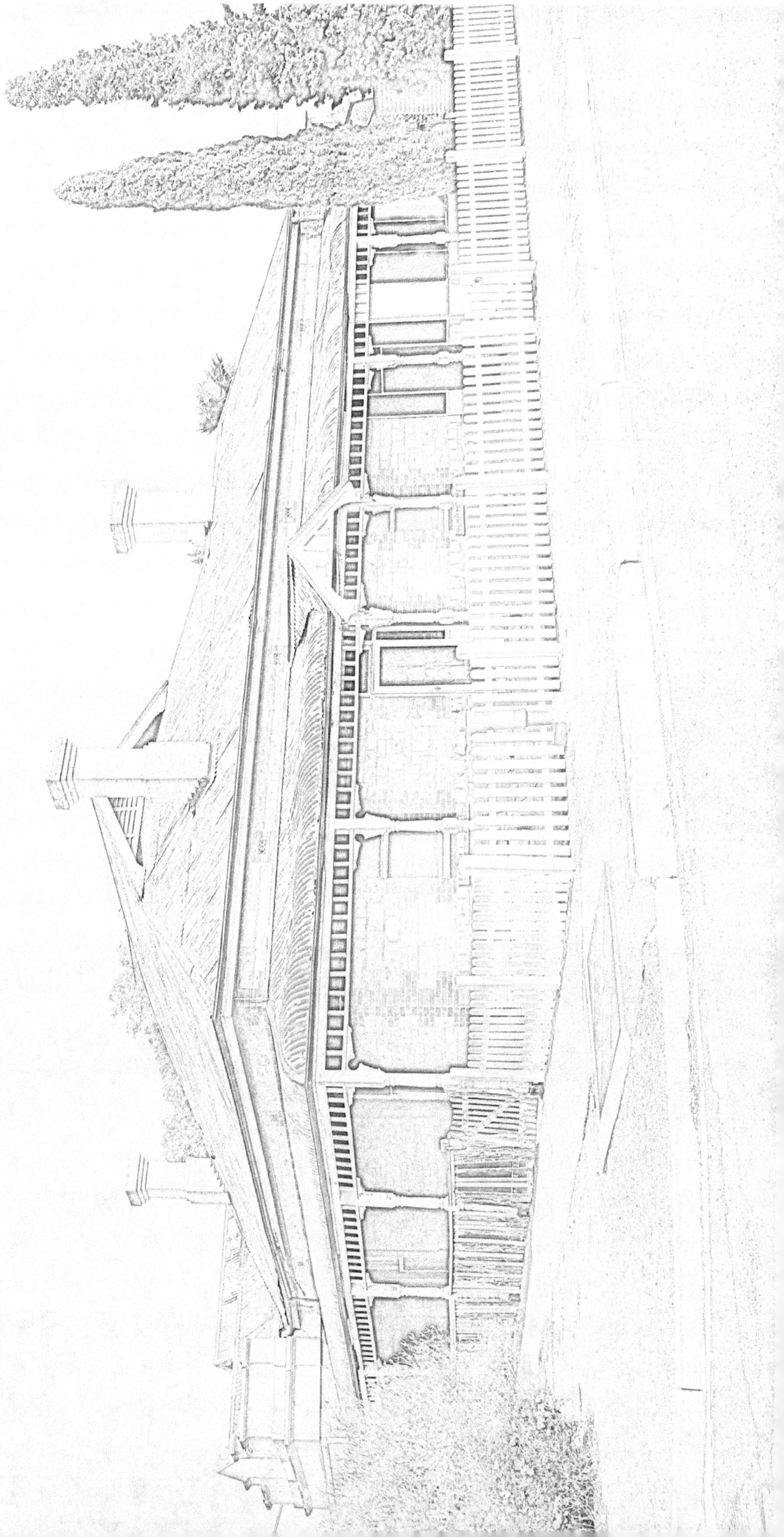

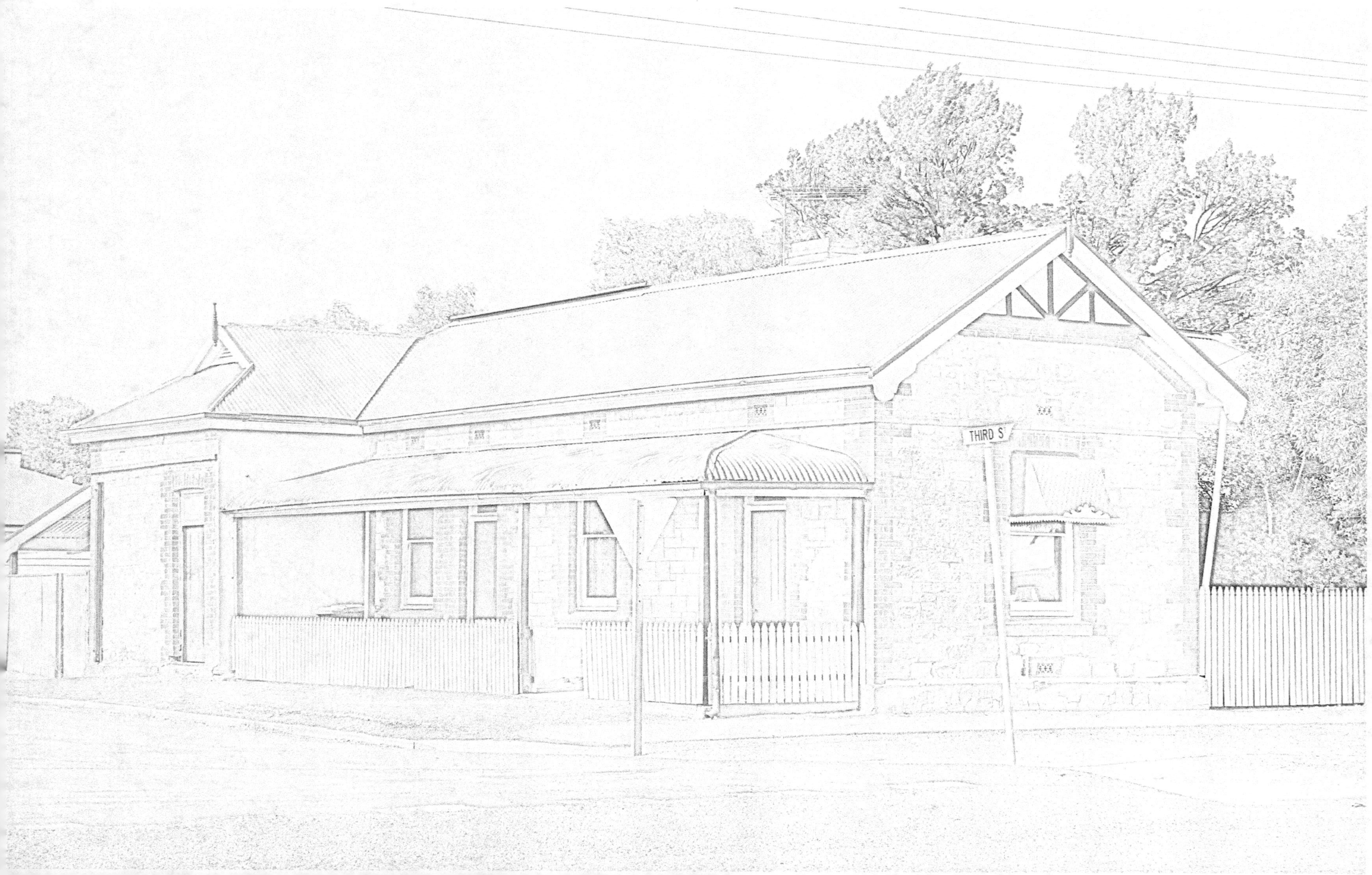
THIRD S

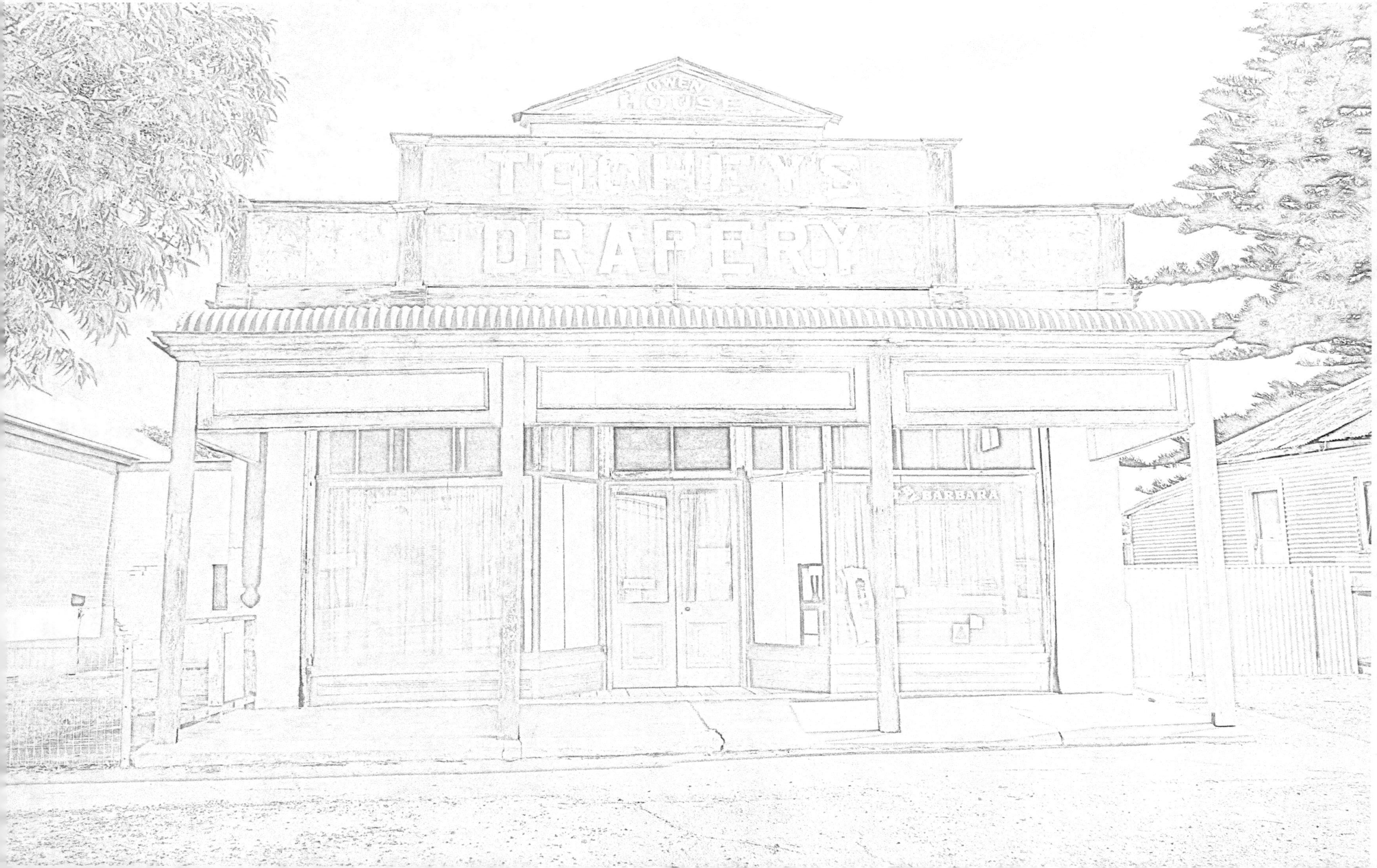
OWEN
HOUSE
DRAPERY
BARBARA

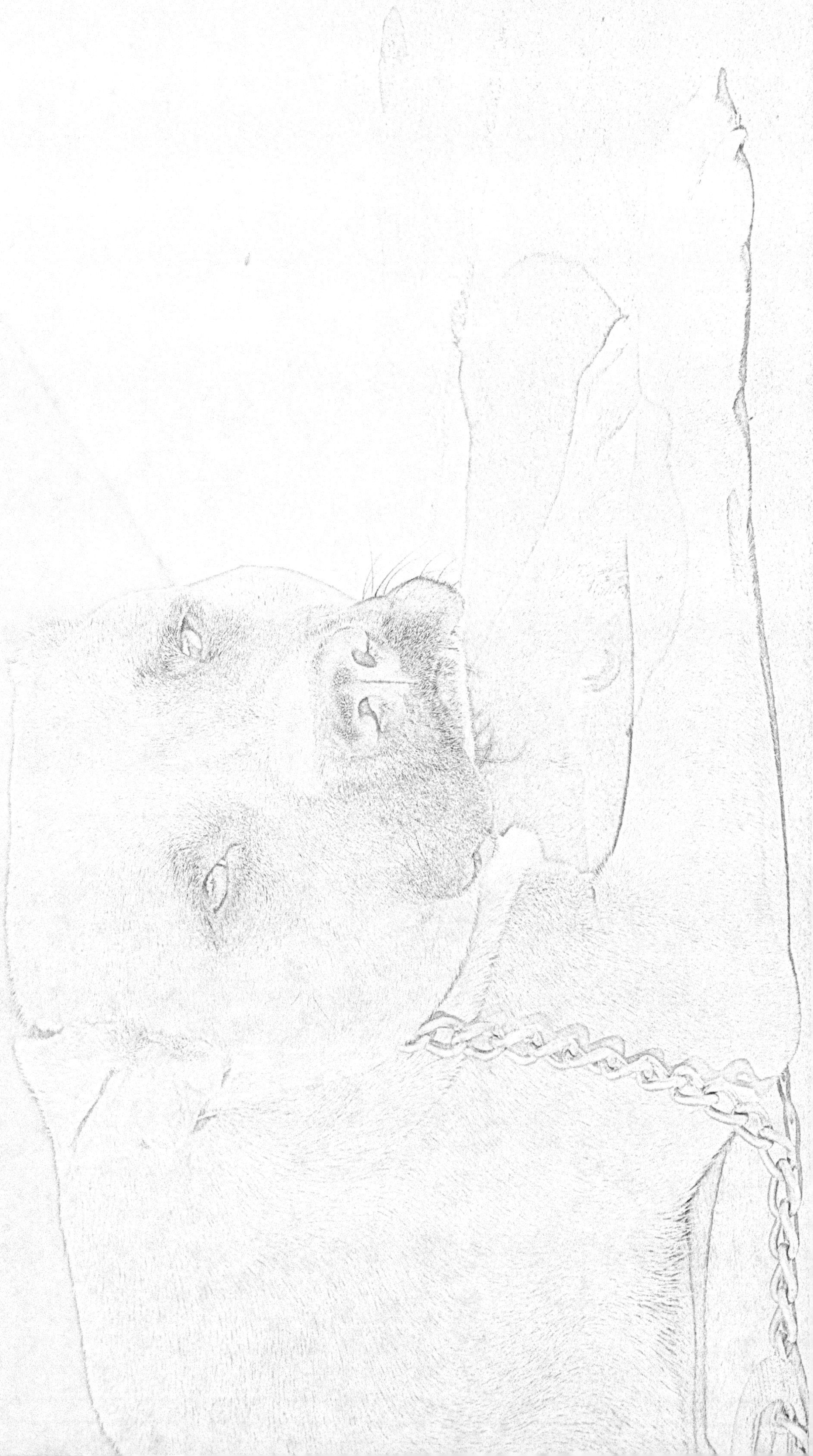

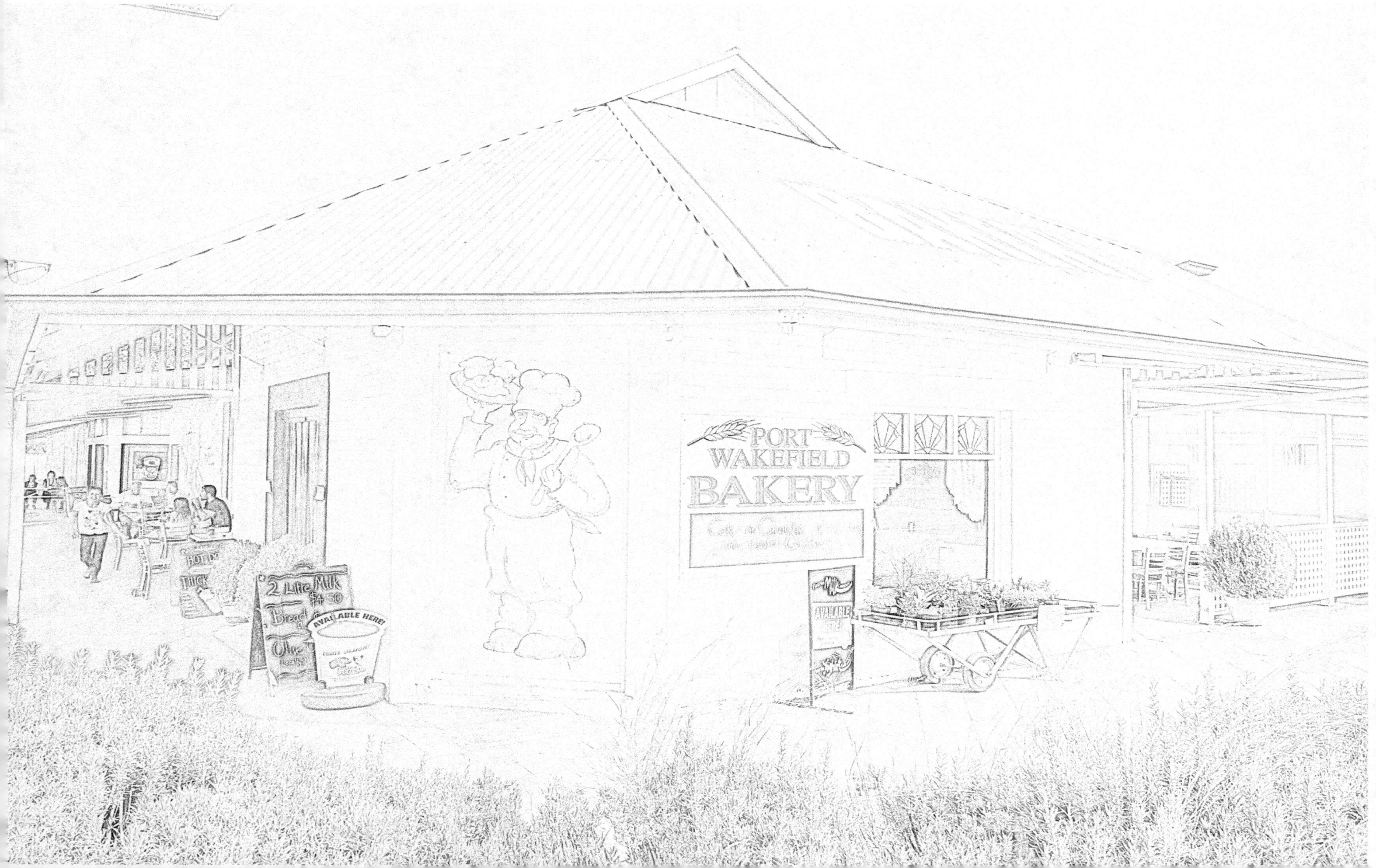
PORT
WAKEFIELD
BAKERY
2 Litre Milk
$4.50
AVAILABLE HERE!

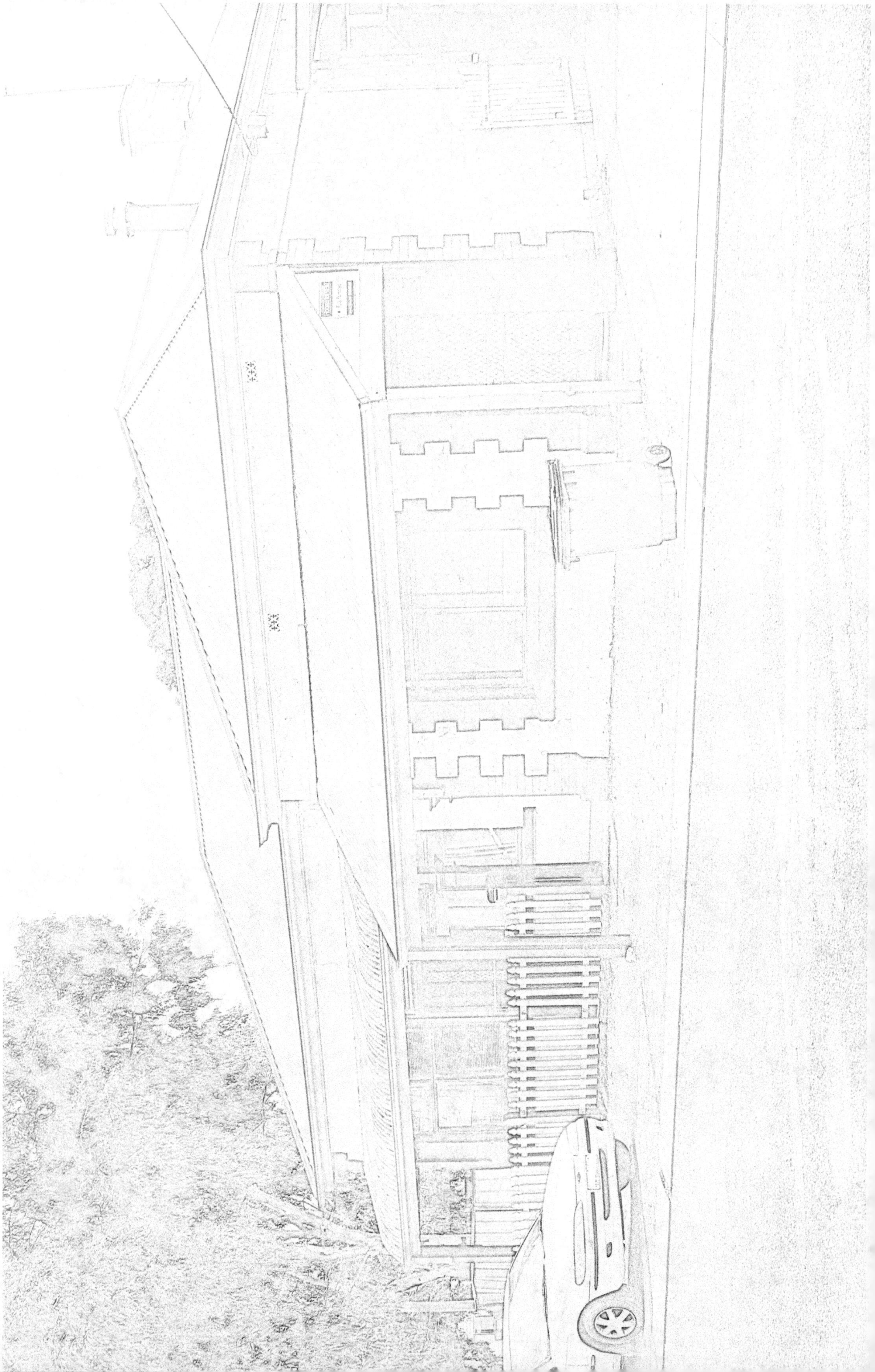

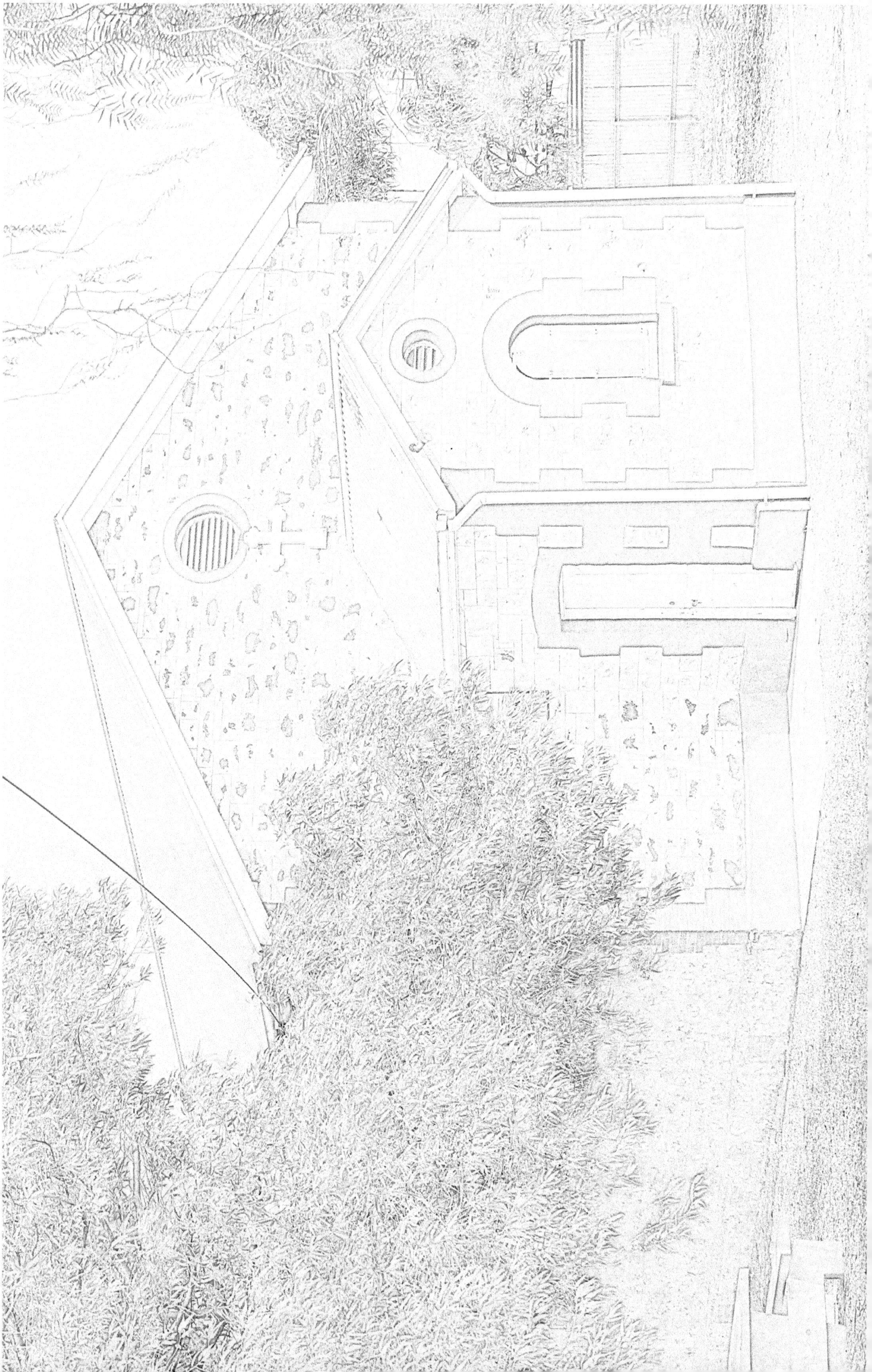

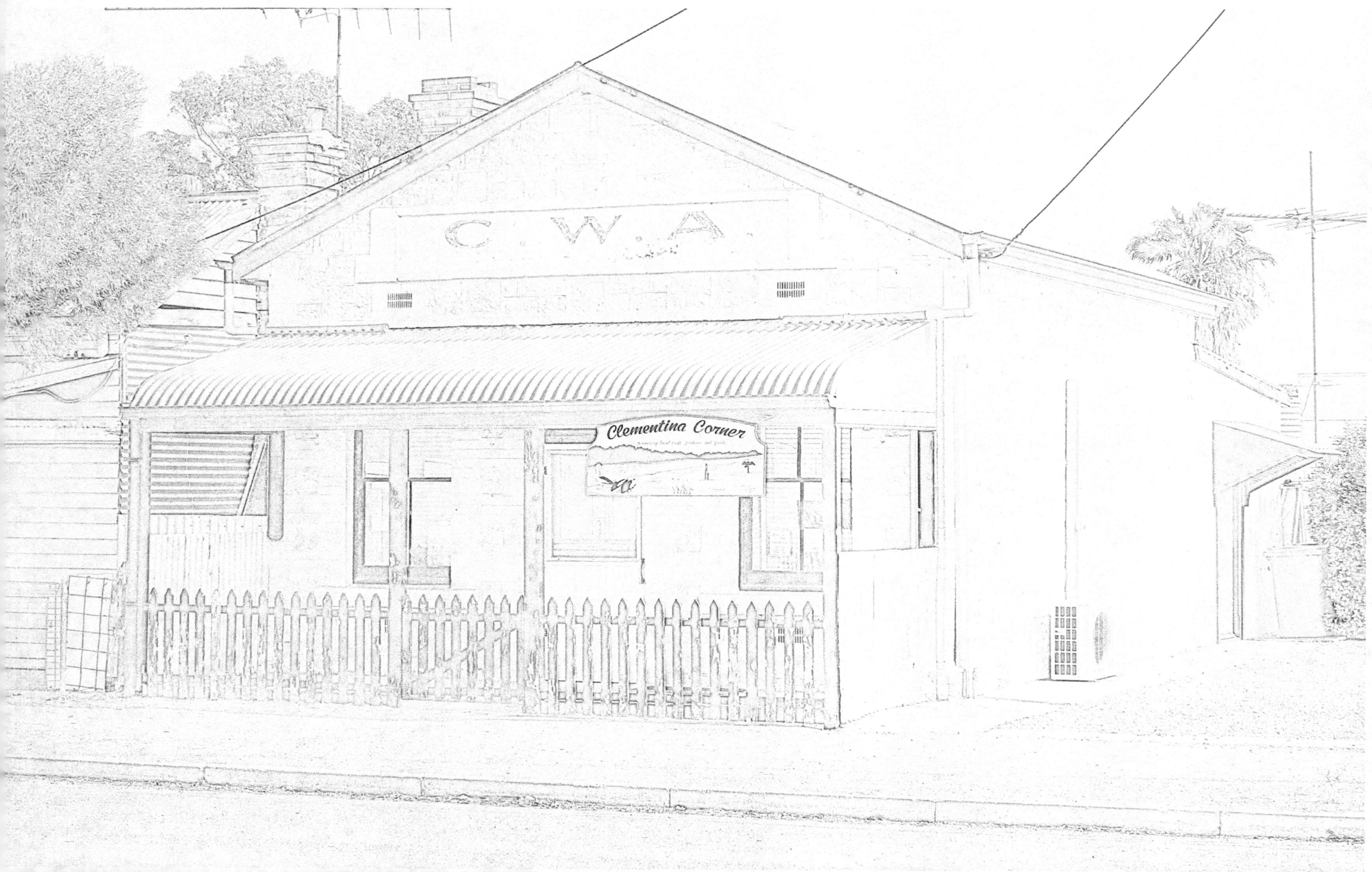
C.W.A
Clementina Corner

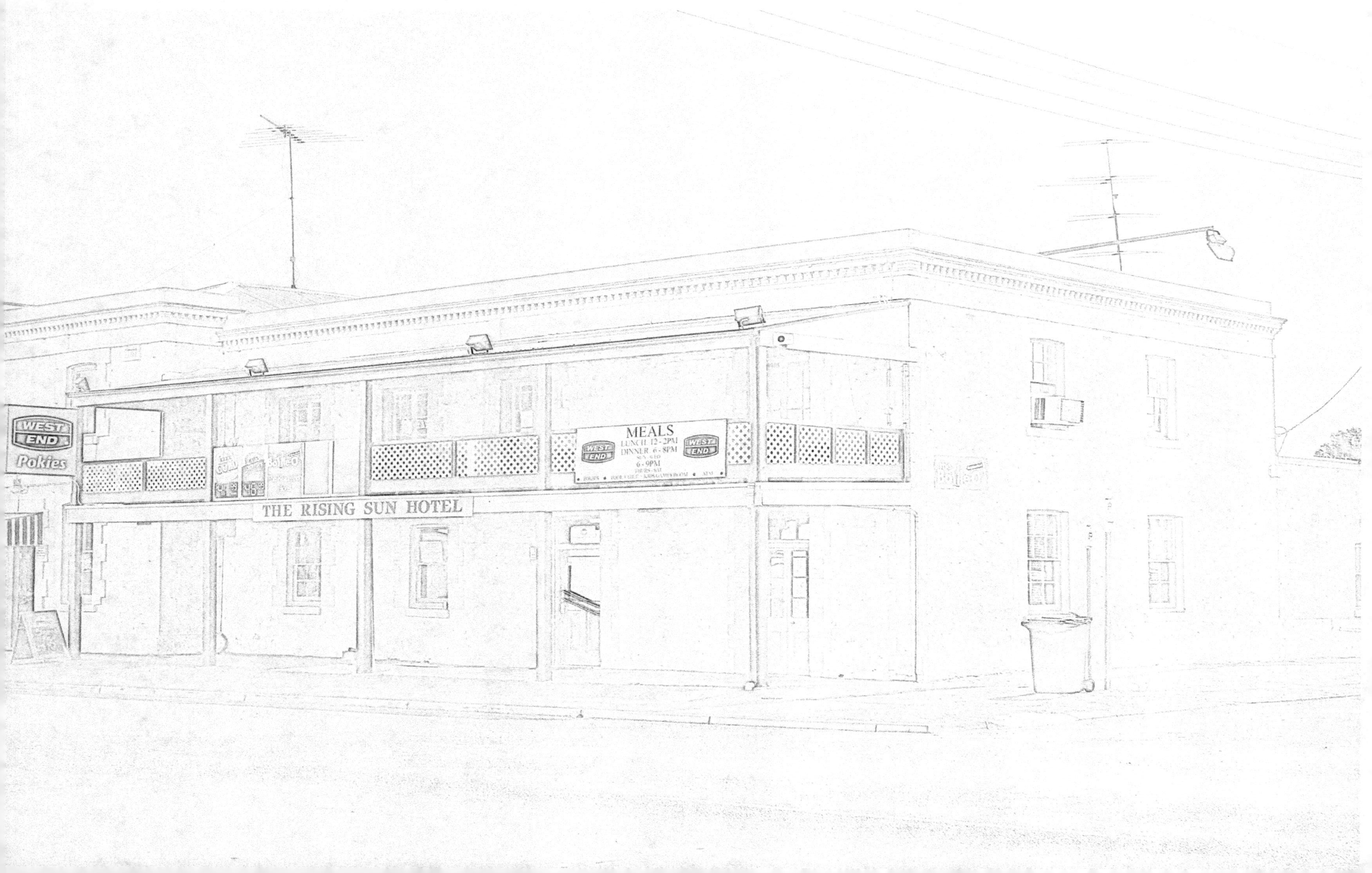
WEST END
Pokies
THE RISING SUN HOTEL
MEALS
LUNCH 12 - 2PM
DINNER 6 - 8PM
6 - 9PM
WEST END
WEST END

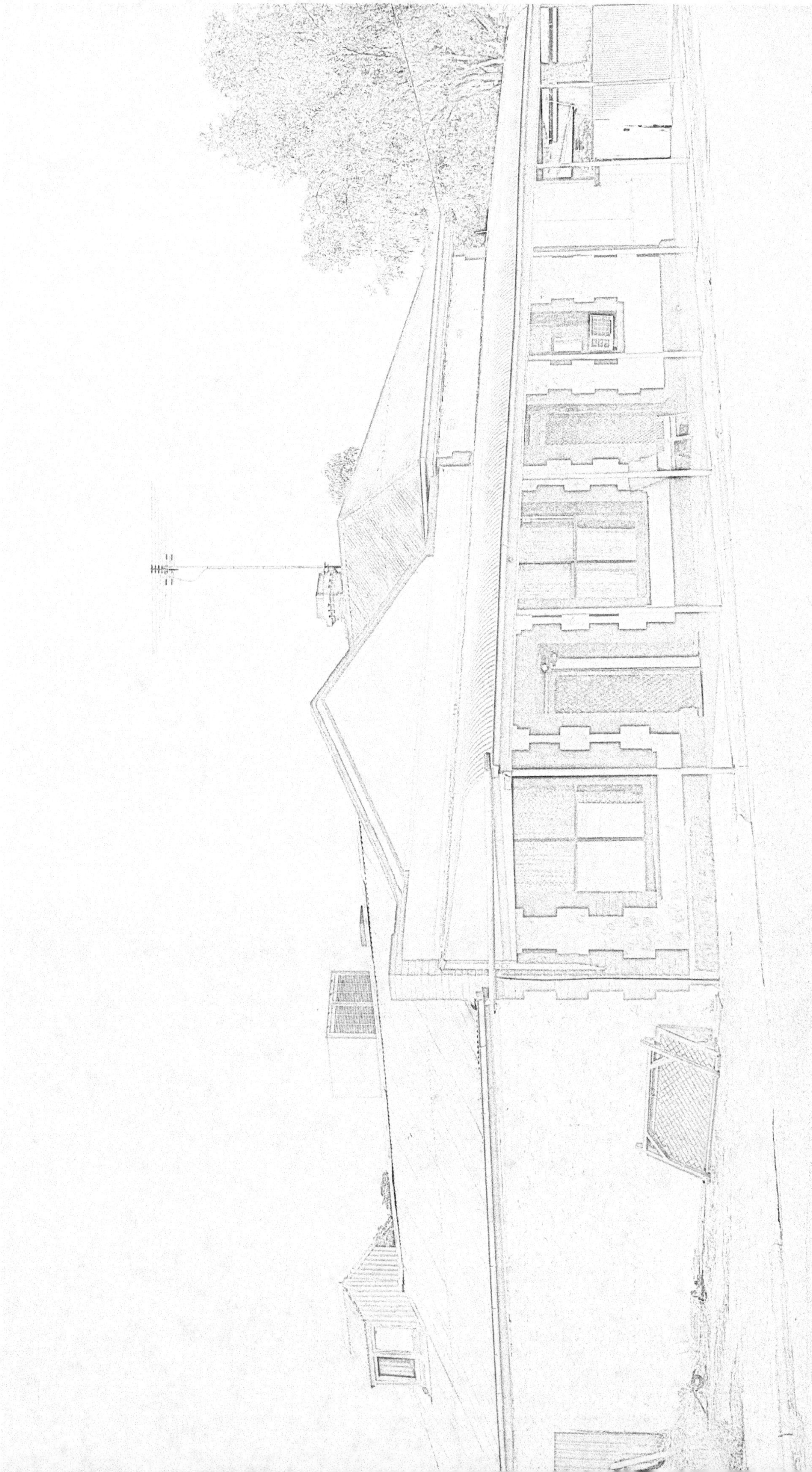

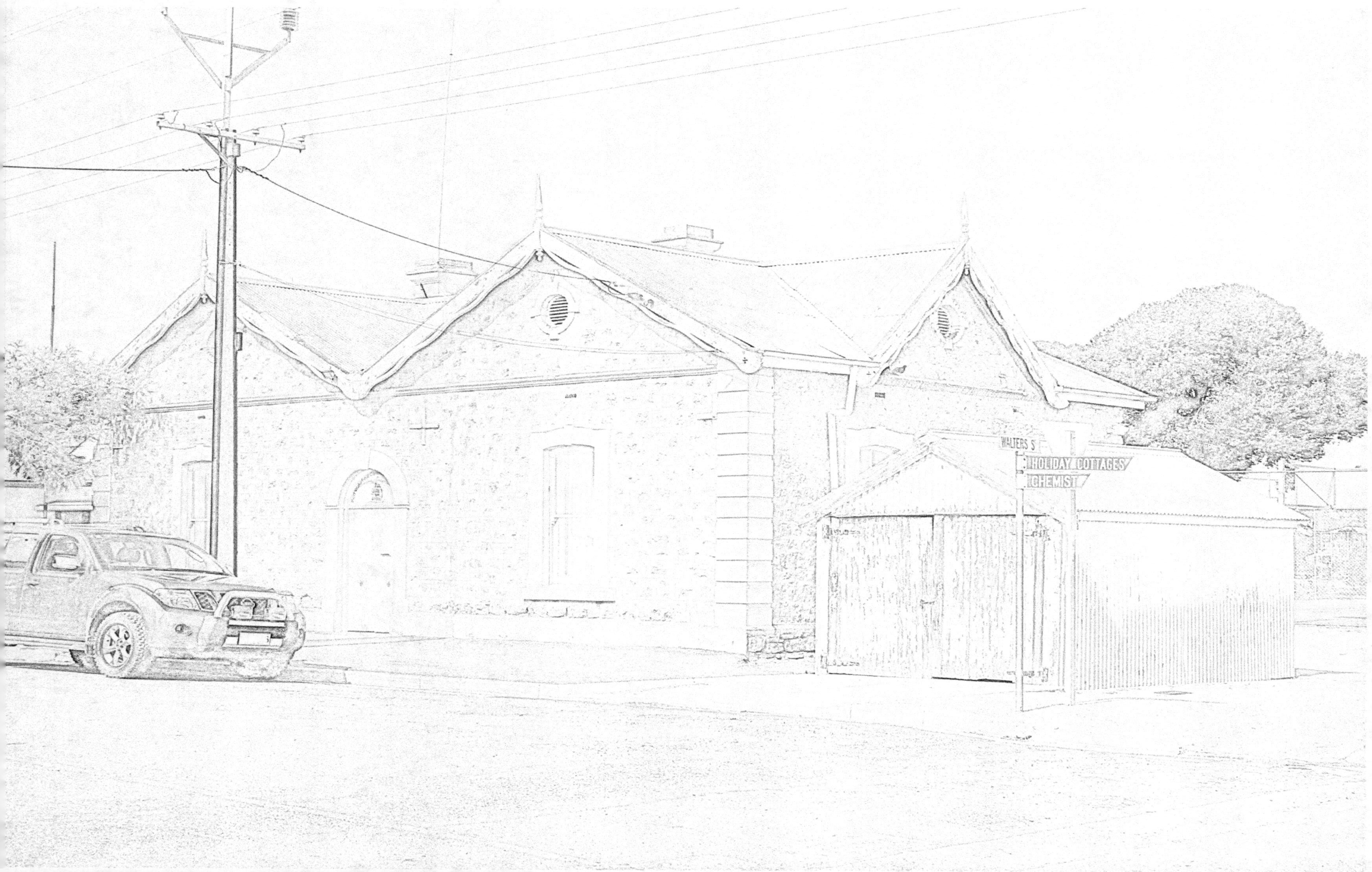
WALTERS S
HOLIDAY COTTAGES
CHEMIST

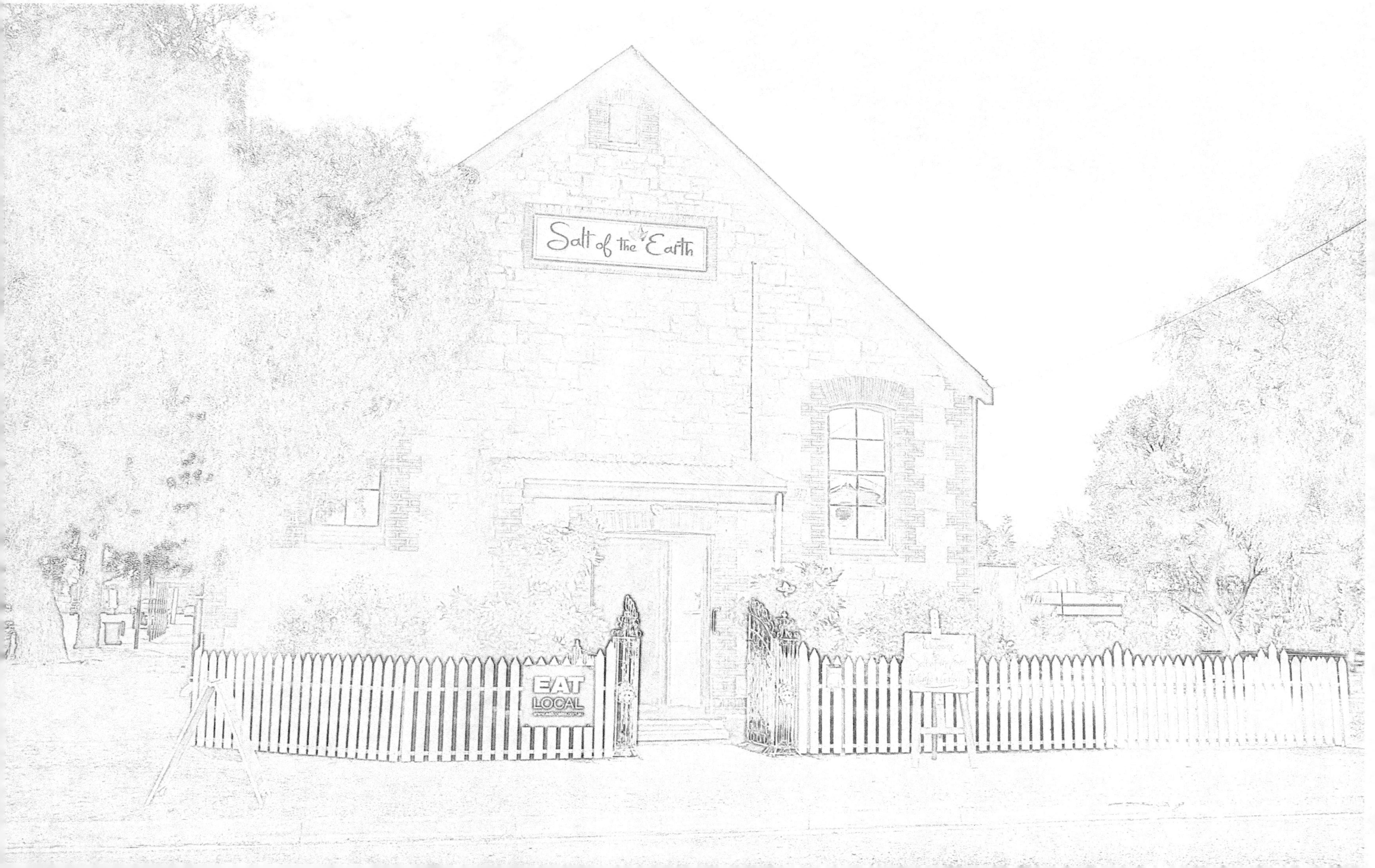

Salt of the Earth
EAT
LOCAL

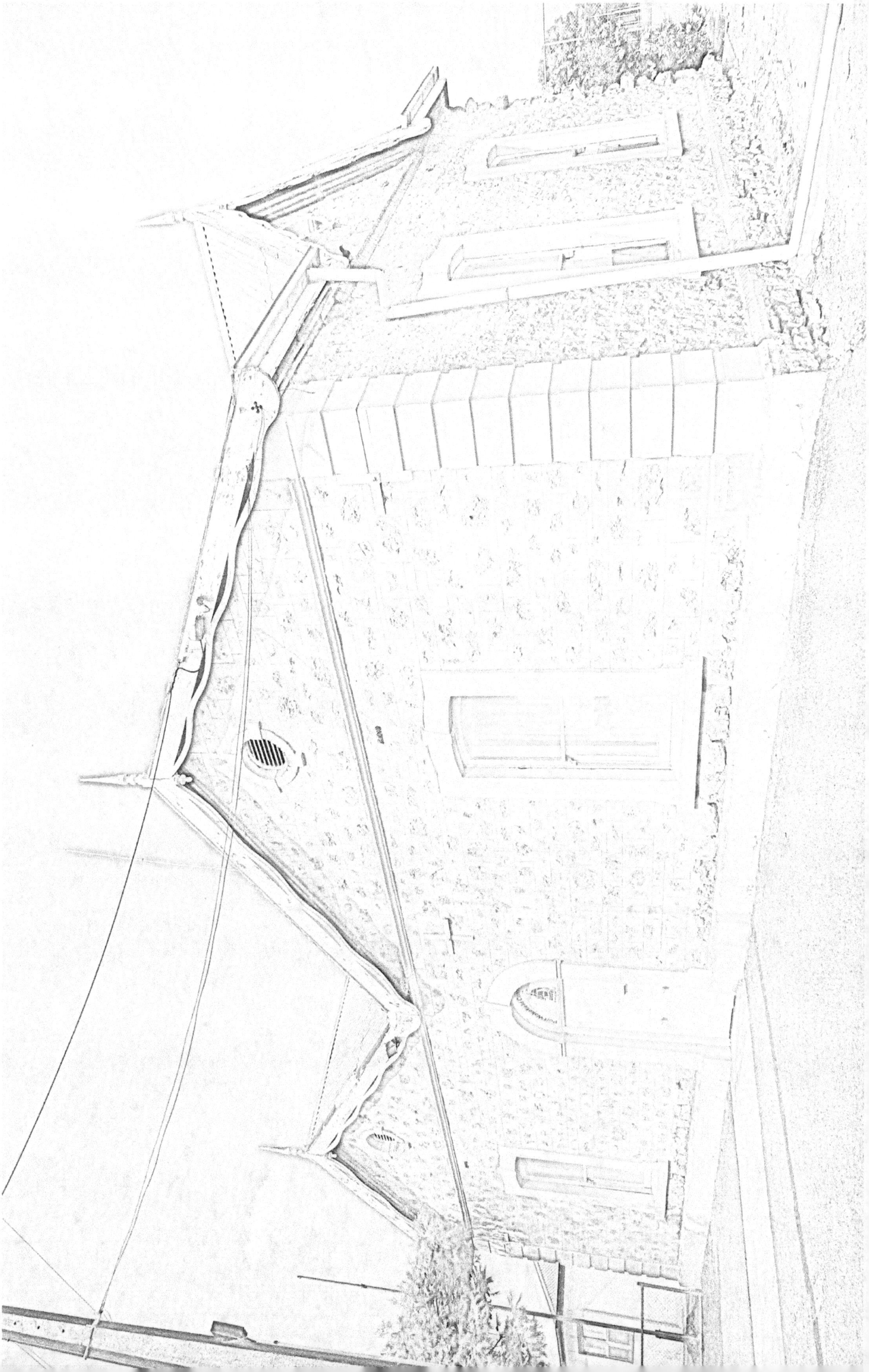

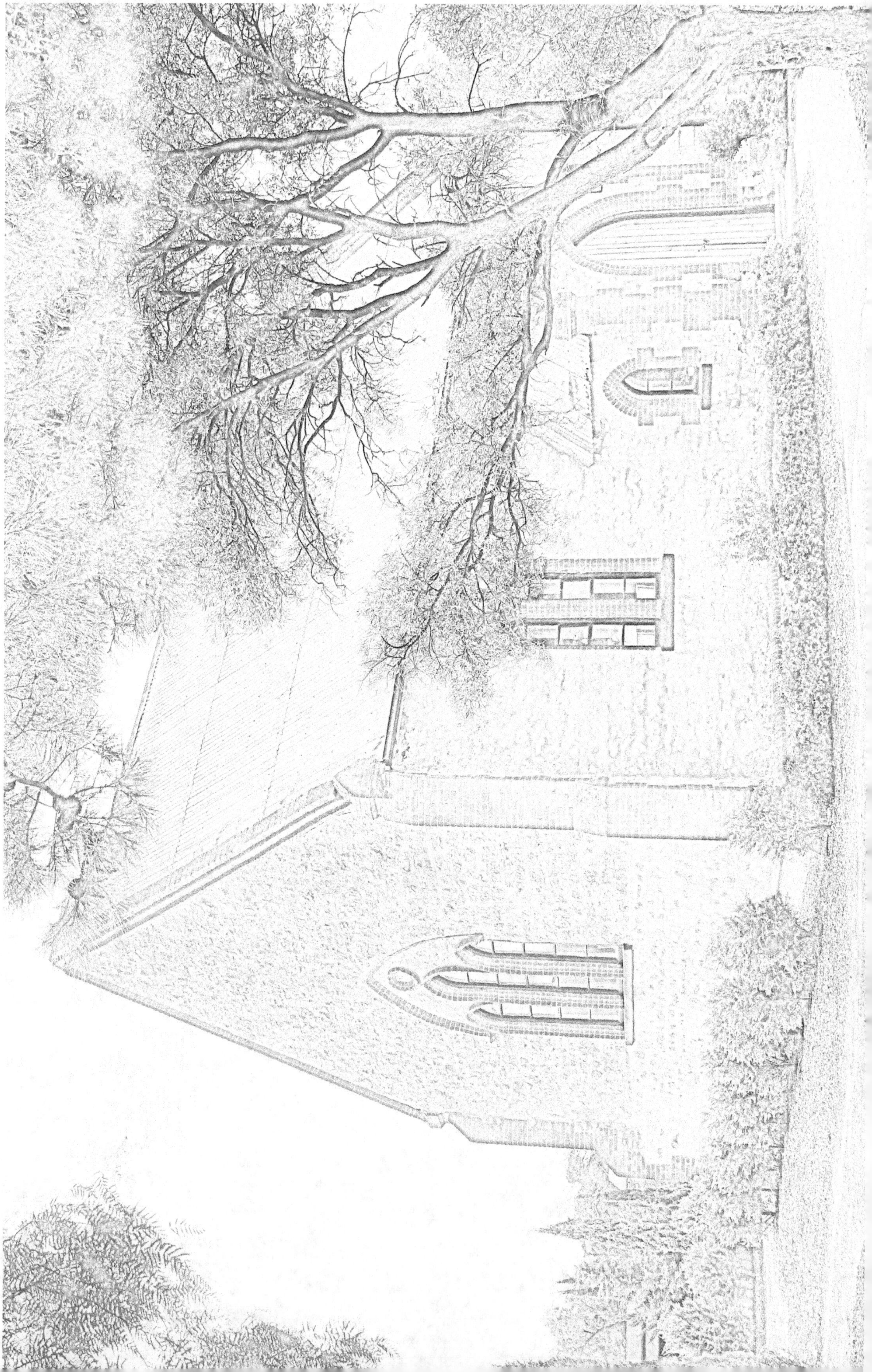

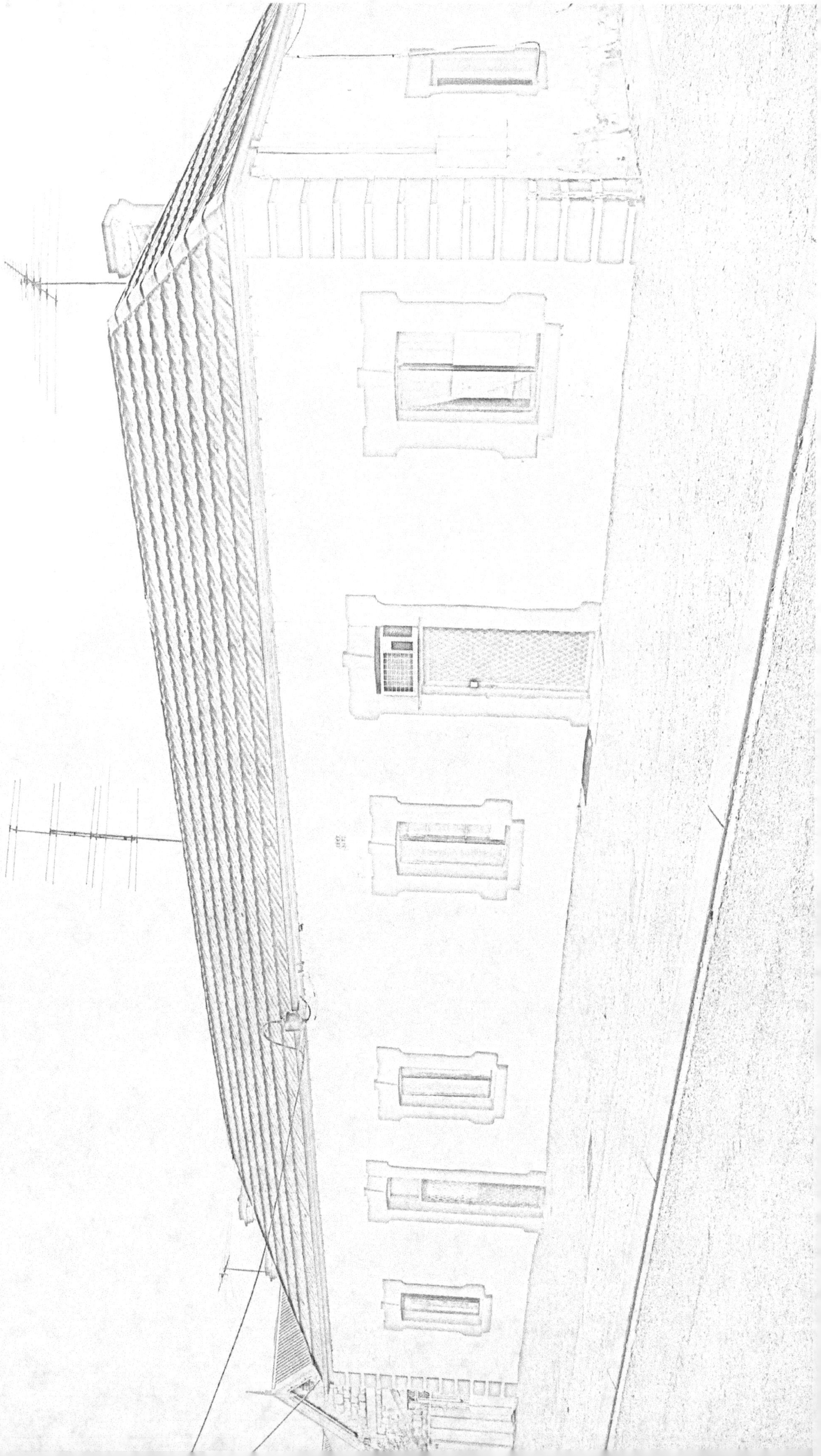

www.ingramcontent.com/pod-product-compliance
Lightning Source LLC
Chambersburg PA
CBHW081047180526
45170CB00005B/1730
* 9 7 8 0 3 5 9 9 7 2 3 3 3 *